God Gets The Glory!

"Angry Tears"
Who Will Wipe My Angry Tears Away?

My Testimony
Revelation: chapter 21 verse 4

Written By:
Evangelist Earlina Denise Gilford-Weaver

To order additional copies of this book, contact:
Xlibris
1-888-795-4274
www.Xlibris.com
Orders@Xlibris.com
736116

Table of Contents

I

Dedicate This Book Too My Lord
and Savior Jesus Christ

I wrote this book in the Memory of my
Big Brother Curtis A. Wright"

01/15/56-10/25/85

What can I say about Curtis my oldest brother, aka Te-bone"
well he is a solid rock, your life here on earth help me to seek
the plan & purpose God has for me, to be a Protector to my
children the way you were to me, I was able to know I was
loved through your drive you had in being a big brother, I
know god called you home for his plan, and I had to grow to
know this but every day i wished I had a call, a visit, or one
look and holding your hand to know that it is okay to trust
and live again, so you helped me grab onto god unchanging
hand, miss you so much.

Special Thank You Too'

My Husband, "Richard A Weaver" for being who you are and being a proud husband' I Love You.

My Babe Sister Snetha Davis you got a story to tell! Tell it!!!

My Children that love me through it all!!! I Love You, Theresa, Floyd, Jermaine,

Memory I miss you Family

My Father Richard Gilford, A man that always showed his love in a way no one could, or would understand through his pain I gain Life to Live and Fight for who God has me to be.

My Mother Theresa Wright-McKnight, Love this lady for who she was, forgave her for what she did, and cared for her because she was my Queen,

My Grandmother Katie Mae Wright a wise woman, a woman that could calm a storm when needed, taught me the meaning of being a respectful woman, and to seek God through it all.

To my Special Mother that God sent my way Corneisha Jones, a woman that gave me a family, who told me to make a stand for something, and never fall for anything,

My Baby Brother Lamont "Buck" Dent, my baby brother that I miss that kept me smiling in ways I never could, who is gone to young, for a reason only God knows, his was the sparkle in my eye and heart.

Mother Williams, A Woman of Virtue, who was a wonderful rock, helped me to appreciate my own Mother through the storms & past, who could find a Virtuous Woman, I did God sent me her way, I Miss you

To My Family & Friends who played Apart' of my Healing

My Aunt Pat, A strong women that show me how to live through loving who I am' showed me to be a mother to my children and has always been a special Queen to me

Minister Burt Williams for just being a good friend in time of need and speaking the word back into me!

My Adopted Brother & Sister's Leslie Scott & Jennifer Johnson, Sam Jones I Love you for allowing it to be easy to be your family!

To My All My Grandbabies- Shekinah, Manuel, Braylin, Nevaeh, Sayvion

My Sister's in the Lord that believed in the Ministry in me & Support me through the hard times, Playwriter Mary Boyles, Latasha Dendy, Renee Newman, Andrea Southard,

My Spiritual Children that I love more than just words, Angela Duckett-Sharper, Dorian Thomas,

My God Children – Mercedes Williams, Shateka Merchant, Elaijah Bennett, Jareal Burger

My Best Friends/Sisters for Life Minister Rochelle Dawson & Mary Boyles

To a very special Daughter in Law' but I say my Daughter Ebony M. Ellis that I love who is an awesome mother

To my very special cousins I love dearly,

Elizabeth Brown, James Carter, Caroline Cole-Lucus

To My Spiritual Mentor Family That God has sent to lift me when I want to quit, to love me and help me in ways that only God knows, a true anointing of deeds and not just in words, D'Atra Hicks, Mr. Prince Zaire, Alene Wilson-Harris, David E. Talbert, Attorney Lori Shells

Mr & Mrs David & Hiltrud Walker a Mighty great team Only God"

My sharp, smart, intelligent first born who sacrifice to help the vision of God she saw in me my partner in all God has for us my daughter Theresa Gilford aka TC

To Mr. Brian West a man of humble Love

For all the people that help me jump over the mess by being the mess! It isn't over until God says it's over!!

To My Spiritual Father Bishop Jenkins, that has always been there for me whenever I needed him, who has loved me in that way that makes me know God is real, I will always be so grateful for you

To the ministries that the lord had in me all the time, for giving birth right when I needed a friend, which restored my soul and gave me true purpose and courage to keep on Standing throw the Angry Tears" the storms & hurricanes which made me a sparkle in the eye of all them tears and a twinkle star in God heart!!!

Angels W/ Extra Blessings, Angels That Give Love, God Chosen Angels, Shekinah Glory Drama Outreach Ministry, 2Real4U Drama Production,

This book is to reach all types of situations, all Youth & Adult, the lost & found, this is life, and I pray this book helps you through any storms in your life, so that you can come out of them hidden dark closets the enemy has hidden you in!

After reading about my life, I hope and pray that this will be a step for you to make toward your victory, and bring you closer to the one and only true love of your life, "Jesus Christ" and to come clean with God and allow him to restore the true beauty that Satan has colored ugly!! So that you will be able to take off that mask of shame, blame, fame, and game! And give God the glory for giving you the power to KNOW WHO IS GOING TO wipe those angry tears away!!!

Revelation: chapter 21 verse 4

Here I go, My Story, My Testimony

Part 1

Chapter 1

Where it all started'

Well let me start my story with the age I could remember, a lot of us like to talk about what People or family have told us, things that happened in our life from their point of view, but the word of God tells us to speak only things that are seen and not things that we really don't know the facts. I don't want to write hear say only the facts, I never wanted to be a false witness to anything rather I believe it or not, so here it goes! I am telling what I know, what I have experience in my life, up until this point. If you got kids put them to bed, if you got company talk to them later, if your phone rings let the answering machine get it, sit in a comfortable seat cut off the TV and be ready to feel that God is real!!

Here it is the truth and nothing but the truth in Jesus Name!

Will Wipe My Angry Tears Away?

I was 8 years old I really never remember my parents only my grandmother and a few aunts and uncles and hand full of cousins. At this time of my life, I was living with my grandmother, she had raised her kids and now some of her grandkids, grandma always took us to church and this is when I started hearing about a man name Jesus and God in heaven that we pray to when we need him, at this time of my age they would tell us to pray for things that we want that are good or something we just wanted God to change. Especially if things are bad! So I always kept this in my heart and mind. I always wanted to know where and who my parents really were, but we really never talked about it, but I did know their names, so I kept a lot to myself. So growing up with a lot of thoughts to me was very hard, because I really never knew how to talk to God about it, especially when I could not see him. So as time went by I was about 9 or 10 years old my grandmother would take us over one of our aunts house to stay a lot because she loved to go to bingo, or night church,

Her and my aunt would go and a couple of uncles would care for us, baby-sit, and their type of babysitting was not good it was bad! They would do bad things to me and my cousins and my little sister, they would come into our bedrooms and touch us in places that were bad places, that my grandmother would say that was precious to God, and they would make us touch them in places that felt bad. Sometimes they would pull our legs apart and put something in, and it would hurt. It would hurt so bad that I would pray to God to make them stop. I would pray all the time to God for it all to go away. Make them stop God, and bring something good because this was bad, it would make me shed tears all the time, but he never did. And it continues on and on and on our uncles would threaten us, telling us that we better not tell, because no one would believe us.

And we would be sent away to strangers that would do worst things to us, because my mother was a prostitute and my father was a drunk and they did not want me

So we kept it to ourselves, me and my cousin would talk about it among ourselves, and I sat up many of nights talking to my little sister about it.

Even my brother could not help me even though he tried so many times, but they were older and stronger than him.

They would beat him up all the time and tell my grandmother that he was bad so he would get in trouble all the time. But my brother never stops trying to help me!

No matter what it cost him! As time went by I started to act bad so God could bring good, then my grandmother started to get sick she was caring for us and it got to be too much for her. And by then I was too much for her to handle and I had a favorite aunt that I was so close too, I use to think she was my mother but she was just my aunt she helped my grandmother with us a lot but that was not enough.

But I was glad to get away from them monsters my uncles.

I am Scared

I started getting visits from a man that was always drunk, I was around 12yrs old then and my grandmother let me know that he was my father but he was scary, but to tell you the truth I did not care, because if I could go with him it would be better than being with around my uncle's.

But my grandmother would not allow him to take me, my grandma would send him off seeing that I was kind of scared of him, and his actions, and there was something he did in the past to me, he had kidnap me and put me in a cage as a baby in a basement, I was told this, but I have memories of this sometimes, being in a very dark place, I don't know how old I was at that time, he would always say I am your father girl don't be scared of me! In a way I was still scared, father or not, his action was crazy.

My grandmother never let me go with him, But as time went on grandma had to let someone else care for us, I was scared to go somewhere else, so one day she told us that our mother was coming to get us, I really wanted to meet her, but my brother hated her, and I did not want him to be mad at me so I would act like I hated her too.

Even though I was so sad and wanted my mother to take me away from the monster's in the my grandmother house, and she needed some rest, at this time I was around 13 my brother was 16 my baby sister was 11, my brother would get into so much trouble that it got him sent away for a while just so he would not go with our mother,

But I love my brother so much I did not want to hurt him, so I would do what he did and say what he say, but our grandmother said we had to go with her even though we said we did not want to go, grandma was tired but me and my sister went with our mother, So I would protect my sister like my brother would do me and let my mother boyfriend's touch me instead, I cried and cried and cried for God to please save me. Since God did not help I had to do anything so they would not hurt my baby sister.

My mother would come home and I would tell her that I did not like her boyfriend because they were bad and mean to me and my sister, she would get mad at me like she hated me and would tell me to stop lying,

I was not going to mess up her life, I better be glad she came and got me and if I keep lying then she was going to send me away, one day she slapped me across the face with a hot comb that you straighten your hair with, because I kept telling her what they would do to me. So I just stayed quiet and kept what ever happened to me to myself, I got beat every time her boyfriends said I was mean to them. So I let them do whatever. I knew if I fought back like I did I would get beat any way or I would get killed, I see why my brother hated her where is this God my grandmother said you can pray to when things get bad?

I guess this was not bad enough for God to hear my prayers, so as time went by, I got rebellious and act up, I hated my mother all she cared about is money and her men, it seemed like they would give her money just to leave the house so they could rape her daughter, I wondered if she knew and just did not care, or what?

So I started stealing, lying and talking back to my mother and I would runaway all the time,

It seem like the streets were safer than grandma house and my mother house, finally I got into so much trouble that it leaded me into being awarded to the state, where they placed me into a juvenile detention home since God would not help my tears that became angry tears to stop maybe the courts would. I stayed in group homes until I got into foster care and went into about 23 different places in all, I was about 15 thru the 16 years old and believe me it was only 3 good homes I had out of all the foster care homes that was okay to live in.

I had to endure so much abuse such as name calling because I was dark skin, beatings because of other people kids, sexually & mentally and being raped by these so called foster mothers husbands, boyfriends & brothers, sometimes their uncles or their older sons. Sometimes I would not eat they would send me to bed without dinner at times, I had to clean up the whole house by myself, I had got into lots of fights with their children because they would talk about my mother and father,

For some strange reason I could not explain why I would get mad because my parents never cared anything about me, If they did they would not allow these things to happen to, but in my heart I loved my mom and dad and wanted dearly to have an relationship with them, strange but real. I can remember this one foster home I got sent to I was about 14 and it was in Canton Ohio, I was happy to go their maybe because it was not in the hometown I stayed in, and I thought maybe the people would be different maybe only bad things happen where I lived and God would help me somewhere else,

This home was big and nice the foster parents had three children two girls and one boy one was around my age, for about one month everything was great I was so happy, God heard my cry, because every night I would get scared and the foster mother would come and hold me and wipe my tears away with a purple small cloth, I was so scared to get close to her, I was scared to love her or her kids, I loved the one foster sister I had,

She was so nice we would go to church together and sing in the choir it was so nice, then one day I came home from church and my make believe family became a nightmare my foster mother wanted me to go in the basement and do the laundry for her, she had to go to store,

and my one foster sister went with her and my foster brother was out with his friends and my one foster sister was in her room, she was a special need child, she had Autism, so she stayed in her room a lot, so I was left their to care for her, my foster dad always stayed in the basement I never knew why, they never was in the same bedroom,

He was always in the basement working and drinking so he lived down in the basement.

We never had a relationship like my foster mother and foster sibling, so I walked down in the basement and I was singing a song we had learn at church and he ask me to come here, I was not really scared because he never done anything to me and I was living there for about 2 months, so I went to see what he wanted and he ask me to help hold some kind of board down for him and I did,

The started asking me question like do I like boys or men? And I was a pretty black girl, and I had a nice body shape, I was so scared to answer him, I started shaking and told him I had to get back up stairs before they come home, I had to get laundry done for my foster mom, but he grabbed me and said they will not be back for a while, so be quite and stop my crying, he started saying I read your files and you are already damage goods, and no one else would have you, and they would not believe you if you tell my wife, we will send you back from where you came from,

I was so upset with God I did not understand why the lord would allow this to happen in another town. Why did my past follow me here! So here I go again my tears has return I was so ashamed that God never love me enough to not let these tears return. I guess adults just don't know how to love or treat a child like me.

Broken, rejected, neglected, molested, ugly, black, a one big failure, this is all they had seen in me, just a messed up kid and just too much work to keep.

Well I stayed in this foster home for 6 months I starting getting into trouble so much and my foster mother could not deal with it anymore because she said that it would affect her children, so her and the monster in the basement decided to send me away after he suggested that I sleep in the basement, so I would not be poison to his girls, I refuse to sleep down there, and I grabbed a knife to defend myself from going into the basement. So the child protected service people came and they tried to talk to my foster mother to give me another chance, so we talked and I told them why I was acting out because I did not want to go in the basement because her husband had hurt me, just like he said,

No one would believe me, she looked at me with hatred in her eyes and made them take me away! So here I am again going back to the city of death. And into another place where I stayed in, they called me names, cut my hair to make me look like a boy, mentally and physically abuse me, and made me wear ugly clothes, the only time I dressed nice was when the social workers came and do a home visit.

This is the only time I felt pretty on the outside, but after the visit the nightmare on everyone street I stayed with came back. But I had my share of tears that no one ever seen and those were the ones on the inside that no one could get to, not even I could wipe them away. I always remember to pray from my grandmother, I don't know why I did but I always wanted to obey my Grandmother, so I prayed and prayed and prayed till I could not pray anymore for God to please wipe my tears away, then I just gave up on the God my grandmother would talk about. So I tried to kill myself in the group homes they took me too,

By taking a lot of pills I was 15 years old when they put me in a mental hospital. This is when I realize no one would ever be able to will wipe my tears away because now they became angry tears' I felt that I was an unwanted child so why did God allow me to be born? Because I felt I was a child of the devil, I had to be because my grandmother said God loves his children, to turn his back on me like this, I could not be one of his children. Was this my punishment for my mother's mistakes?

For her life not being right and had me? Is this why God could not love me? Or wipe my tears away?

I had no life to look forward to, no one will ever love me unless I allow everyone to touch me in ways I never wanted to be touch. Should I allow them to do this to me so I can get love? I ask God but he never answered me. What kind of God is this that my Grandma said is Love, what is Love? Is it really a thing that you let all men do bad things to you?

I know in the bible when I was little, my grandma always told me that God loves virgins and he will bless me if I keep myself for when I get married, so did God hate me because my uncles did things to me? Was it my fault? I was too young to make them stop, didn't God know this?

I kept telling myself over and over again. If my tears never get wipe then I will drown. So why live to see my life fails? I will never be nothing that is what my mom always said to me, she said women would never be alone or need money if they use what God gave them.

She said that between a woman legs is money to her riches, I hated to hear her talk like that to me, I never wanted my little sister to be raised by her, I always said to myself when I get big I was going to go back and get my baby sister. But God would never allow me to with the way my life was going. Maybe I would have a chance if the drunk that said he was my father come and get me, or if my brother gets out of jail he would come and get me.

It seems like they were the only ones that cared for me, maybe they would wipe my tears away. While I was in the mental hospital it was workers that watch you all the time they kept me so drugged up I really did not know who I was at times. Then one night it was a guy on shift that would always be nice to me, and bring me extra snacks he was nice I thought to myself but deep down inside I knew he wanted something, so I tried to hang myself, I just did not like how he touched me and before it got physical I rather take my life then to allow it to happen again. But it happen any way and the workers would not believe me, because the drugs make you say things that was in your mind,

She was two doors down from my room and she would hear me scream and cry and would come to my room and hold me until I would fall asleep, who was this lady that cared for me? Why does she care? And she would ask the nurses and doctors about me, and how could she take me home, she wanted to be my mother not a foster mother, but my adopted mother. I asked God why she wants a skinny, ugly, black, messed up child with lots of problems' Don't she know what a hot mess I was so emotionally confused, I really did not trust anyone, no adults because I knew they did not love me, so why does this woman want me? So I would not get close to this woman because I was scared to trust again or open my heart up to anyone, even though I wanted love and wanted someone to wipe my angry tears away, but I was scared to be with her especially if she had a husband, or any male friend, brothers, nephews, uncles, sons or even grandfathers or cousins that were men. But at this time she got the information from the child services, but they had located my real father, he was staying with his sister, my aunt wanted me to live with them.

I was glad but scared because I did not know these people at all, but what can be worst go with my real family or try this nice lady at the hospital. But I really had no choice, so they took me to my aunt's house and there was that same man that would come over my grandma house drunk, this man was really my father now wonder I was messed up look where I came from, a mom that was a prostitute and a father that was a drunk. I lived with them for awhile my aunt was so nice I liked her so much, she was an angel in the sky in my eyes, but she was gone a lot because of her religion, I had lots of cousins and me and my cousin the girl was very close we did a lot together my father drank so much, we really never spent time together, I did not like the way his breathe smelled he was always trying to kiss me and call me my mom nick name he had for her. Ressa Mae" My father was there to watch us a lot but I did not care we had a lots of freedom.

Finally I got to see my brother he was eighteen and he fought to look for me, he was looking all over for me, he was locked up a lot, and he stayed into lots of trouble because he had no one, he never knew who his real father was and my mother cared less, so he hung with the wrong crowd of people. He had an older girlfriend and he was doing okay, he bought me so many clothes and other things, my brother loved me so much and asked me all the time was I happy and I told him yes, because my auntie was great. I was about 15 years old I had 8 more months before I turned 16, my little sister was still living with our mother in New York I was so scared for her, I knew what my mother had done to me so I knew my sister was going to be messed up, so I would at least pray for her maybe God would help her.

And if she had any tears he would wipe them away. I was getting sick a lot because I had asthma and it was hard for me to breathe my tonsils were swelling so I had to go in the hospital to get them out.

I was sick one night my father came in drunk and laid down next to me calling me my mother's name he was talking so crazy I got scared but I knew he was out of his mind.

I did not want to believe that my own father would do anything to me, so I would try to push him out of my bed, but he was heavy and strong and my throat was so sore I could not scream for help, he kept on grabbing me hard and then started calling me my mother name again saying I was his wife, no one can have me but him, I tried to lift him off me but he was to heavy I was too weak I tried screaming again, but no one was home every one was at the temple I could not go because I was sick and my father was watching me, my nightmare began again my own father tried to raped me, did he know it was me? He kept calling me by my mother's name. I begged God to kill me, so I took all my aunts painkillers and other pills I could find, I went to the hospital and they pumped my stomach what is God's problem? Haven't I suffered enough?

I ended back in another group home. I was there for about three months. And that real nice lady came and got me, and told me that no one else would ever hurt me again and she had adopted me she was my mother and everything was going to be okay, and for some strange reason I believed her.

She told me that child services had called her and asked her if she still wanting to adopt me I was 16 and would be 17 in 3 months what do she want with me I was too big for anyone to want me, I wanted to go with my brother he was old enough but because of his back ground and criminal record they would not let me go stay with him. So I went with the nice lady. I was bitter with life; mad at the world I did not care about anything anymore I was so sad I did not want to smile there was nothing to smile about everything in my life was dark.

All the tears I have was flowing in the inside, my heart was drowning, so I went to my new home, my case worker said it will be better this time, I heard this so much I was wondering who was they fooling their self,

Because they was not fooling me, the house was nice she had beautiful things, she have two boys and two girls one my age and the others were younger and they were happy to have me. I was still full of anger and did not trust anyone especially boys and men's, but I said if it happens again I don't care because my body was numb, I just did not care anymore.

The home was exciting lots of family and friend in and out just like a family that was normal. I fitted right in, me and my adopted sisters were great together never fought just was crazy about each other, I loved my little adopted sister and little brother just like a real family I always wanted. We played, cried, and act bad all together, never a difference was made between us, no man in the house, that was great just my adopted mother had a male friend, but she never let him stay at the house, she had brothers they came and left they were nice, when she yelled at me she yelled at her kids the same.

When she spared the rod on me she did her kids, called me names and put me on punishment just like she did her kids, they got it more than me, she would spoil me a lot, I was so happy to be in a normal home, but still had angry tears that would not go away, No matter what and how my new family tried to wipe them. Even through my grandma house had monster's in it, I loved being with my grandma because she never used bad words at us, she took us to church to learn how to be right and love each other and learn about a man name Jesus who died for my sins, and I missed her,

But she was to sick and got too old to raise us, I was not mad at her I loved her, I wanted to tell her so much what my uncles did but I was too scared to let her know, my cousins never said anything to her or my little sister, so I kept my mouth closed,

But I did tell my adopted mom everything she tried to wipe my tears away but it was too many and so much going on inside, it was hard for me to feel her wipes. Maybe this is how people raise their kids I thought.

Call them bad words and names, beat them when they act up, I don't really know but I did not care, I stayed here until I got 17 and believe it or not no one ever touched me in a bad way, my adopted mother said to me if any one try to touch me let her know, and she would kill their behinds. She was tough and no one messed with her, not even her sisters or brother's and she had her man in check. So it was a normal family to me, the best I can ask for. So I did not care about going to church or pray to a God that never heard or seen my tears, my adopted mother took care of it for me. My father would try to come see me, still drinking and acting crazy,

She never let him get close to me or see me, not even my real mother she made sure she protected me from all danger, my real brother always came to see me they loved him and excepted him as family. He was just like another son and my adopted brothers and sisters were his family, they treated him how they did me. I guess this is love.

Maybe everyone shed tears, so my tears did not matter, but inside I felt something was missing I really wanted to see my real mother no matter what she had did, I loved her for some crazy reason, I loved my adopted mother but she was not my real mother.

And I did not what to hurt her feelings by telling her I wanted to see my real mother and my little sister so bad, I just wanted to know if my little sister was okay, I always told her I would protect her and be there for her. I was scared she was going through what I have been through and who was there to wipe her tears away? This time I was being stable and it seemed like God was letting me off the hook, maybe he cared for me enough to stop the pain in my life & the tears from falling.

Even though everyone at this home seemed to love me and treat me so well, sometimes I was treated better than her own children.

Now it is 1976 and I got myself pregnant, by a guy I was sneaking off seeing, and did not know what to do in case something like this ever happens?

How do I handle it? Or should I feel anything? I was so scared, so I hid it from everyone I was 17 years old at this time and was going to be 18 years old in 5 months, I kept it to myself, so I decided to runaway before anyone finds out. Where would I go? So I started asking my adopted mother could I go see my real mother but she kept telling me no, then one day she told me yes, so my real brother did not like our real mother but he knew I wanted to see her so he wanted to make me happy.

So we went looking for her, she was living on the other side of town with a new man and my little sister, she had moved back from New York. And was living here for a while, I guess she did not care to find us, but we found her, And she was living in a real nice home and had lots of nice stuff, I was mad and my brother hated her so much, he was not talking to her he went back and sat in his car while I visit her and my sister.

My little sister was 15 years old, and my mother looked so nice and pretty how can a nice looking lady be so ugly inside

I asked myself? We talked okay' but she was nasty & cold to me,

My little sister wanted me to see her room so I did, she had a nice room better than I ever had or imaged, she had nice cloths and lots of toys, I was kind of jealous of her and felt a little hate, but it was so nice to see her, so I shook it off, then as we were leaving her room she grabbed my hand and said please spend the night with me, it was not what she said, but how she said it! I felt scared for her she had that fear tear voice I know very well, this kind of voice I had, so I told her I would be back if our mother let me stay. So we went down stairs and a man walked in the door he was looking at me like he wanted something, I felt his spirit was not right so I ask my mother could my sister spend the night with me, she said no' I don't like that lady you live with, in a very nasty voice. So I ask could I spend the night before my mother could answer that man did, he said sure you can, you can stay as much as you want to, looking at me like I was something to eat.

So when my brother took me back I told my brother I believe something was going on with our little sister, he act like he really did not care,

My brother always hid his feelings, he never talked to me about our mother past only that he hated her' and that would make me so sad. So we got back over my adopted mothers house and I asked her could I spend the night over my mother's house she said no, I begged her and she still said no, but I was so scared for my little sister I could not put her teary voice out of my head, so I decided to runaway to live with my real mother, plus I was scared to let my adopted mother know I was pregnant anyway, so I left the house that night I had to be about three or four months along, but I wore big cloths from head to toe, I did not want to dress like a girl or nice, because I was scared someone might want sex from me, so I dressed like a boy all the time, with big clothes on so no one knew I was pregnant, so I arrived at my real mothers house and she answered the door I told a lie so I could stay,

I told her that my adopted mother brother was trying to mess with me, so she let me stay blaming me that I must of did something to make that happen and threaten me if I acted up at her home I would be gone in a heartbeat and she better be getting a check for me since my adopted mother was getting one for me, with her nasty looking boyfriend staring me up & down like a piece of meat, My little sister had a big smile on her face my mom and her man talked about it and he said I could stay because it was his house. So I went into my sister room and put my things up that I had with me, my mother said we need to go get you some new cloths because I looked a hot mess, I told her that was okay but she said you need to look like a woman not a man, you need sexy cloths but I did not want her to see that I had a little stomach, cause she would know that I was having a child. So my sister and I went in her room and talked, I asked her did that man ever touch her? But she was to scare to tell me the truth she would tear up and say no, but I knew he had to do something.

So I told her I was about to be eighteen in about 5 months and she could come and live with me. We went to sleep talking, nothing happen that night but a lot of arguing between my mother and that man. I was there at least a week I was sad because I did not want to hurt my adopted mother so I wrote her a letter to let her know why I really left and I love her and I will be back to see her. So as time went on two weeks my mother took me shopping but I act like I was sick, I did have asthma so I act like I could not breathe so she took me home.

That night she had to go to work and left me and my sister home with her man, I did not like his short bright skin self' he was so ugly and thought he was sharp. He calls my little sister in his bedroom and she was scared so I went with her, he asked me what do I want? I said nothing, I am just here with my sister so you can tell her what you want in front of me, he got mad and told my sister to leave and I stay. He got up and closes the door and said if I want to be living here I had to earn my stay like my sister.

I did not care what he did to me as long as he did not touch my baby sister so this nasty man smelled like he was drinking because the smell reminded me of my father, he grab me and starting touching and ripping off my clothes I tried to fight him, I wanted to spit in his face, I hated him and wanted to kill him. Should I tell my adopted mother? She did say she would kill anyone that ever touches me again. Or should I tell my real mother what he was doing to me and my little sister? Well I got sick because he touches me again and he felt something move in me and got up off me and said what is that? I told him I was pregnant. So he did not care, I plotted to kill this man and my mother for allowing this to Happen to us, do she really care?

What's wrong with her? I hated them both so much, I hated my father for being a drunk and allow his craziness to hurt me, I hated all men even God! But not my brother he was different. So my mother found out that I was pregnant and was mad she called me stupid and a hole, said you probably don't know who the father is?

I was okay with the name calling I was use to that with every foster parent and my adopted mother, so I did not care as long as I could stay there to protect my little sister, so my mother went shopping to get me some cloths and baby things, that was the least she could do, I was glad that I was having a baby because someone that I could love and love me back. And maybe my baby will be able to wipe my tears away. I got bigger my brother got out of jail again and found out that I was living with my mother, so he came and got me a lot. He was happy that he was going to be an uncle, he had a son. He was not mad that I was having a baby. I wanted to live with my brother and his girlfriend, she was nice but I was to scare to leave my sister with that man and my mother. I told my brother about what happen to me and he was mad, he went back to my mother's house and beat up the man and pulled a gun out to kill him and my mother, but I beg him not to, because of my little sister. So my mother called the police and they put my brother back in jail. I hated her for this. My brother said he never ever wanted to see my mother again as long as he live even when he die, he said don't let her come too his funeral.

So as time went by my mother man did not bother me or my sister maybe because he had a Girlfriend on the side, and I was getting bigger, or he was scared when my brother got out of prison he was going to deal with him. I was almost due to have my baby and I threaten him if he touch my sister I was going to kill him in his sleep, and that was a promise! My sister and me would go visit her father at his job some center he worked at he would clean in the evening, and my mother needed someone to watch us, since her man decided to leave her for a younger woman, I was glad he was gone, but I felt I was old enough to watch my sister and stay home ourselves, but she was doing something she did not want us around the house to see.

I had my baby it is a girl, she was very pretty I loved her so much, as time went by we was still going to that center and my sister father tried to mess with me, he would offer me money to have sex with him, telling me I look just like my mother and was shaped like her too.

But I fought back this time, I told him I would cut his stuff off if he ever tried to touch me; I fought back for once in my life. I had something to fight for, my little girl. She gave me a reason to live because if something happen to me the things I went through, I thought she would go through, so I was very protected of her, my mother and her new man friend tried to take my baby from me, because he tried to mess with me, my baby was 3months old and I fought him and beat the mess out of him, I grab a knife and cut him I tried to kill his short behind, and my mother slapped me, and I pushed her down, I did not want to hurt her because of my little sister. My sister was 15 years old. So they called the police on me and tried to take my daughter from me, so I ran, I was going to be eighteen in 1 month family services could not touch me then. So I ran back to my adopted mother house she never asked any questions, just took me in like I was her child and protected me. She was not going to let my mother or anyone else take my baby or me. I was back to a place that I called home!

Chapter 2

Now A Mother

I was still hurting and scared for my sister.

And I really did not trust any man at all at this time, I thought about what my grandmother taught me, about saving yourself for the right man, your husband. But I knew that it was too late for me because I was damage goods, so why did this boy like me don't he know that I was damage, so we dated and I met his family he was the only boy and all sisters his mom was nice but crazy, but she did not take any mess, she remind me of my adopted mother very out spoken. Everything that came out her mouth was bad words, she called her kids out their names just like my adopted mother' but she loved them and cared for them, I love them and fitted right in, his mother loved me it was nothing she would not do for me. And he was a good man, he never asks to touch me and we dated for six to eight months before we did anything. The day we messed around he said I was going to be his wife I was eighteen and was about to be nineteen years old when he asked me to be his wife. He was the only boy I ever trusted besides my brother. So we moved in with his oldest sister so I could have a home for my daughter,

I went with him all the time to hear him sing, then right after my nineteen birthday I was sick, I was pregnant again, so we got married and got our own place I finally had my own family. I really believe that this was love because he was the only man I had to sleep with, and he never force me to do anything I did not want to do, we went months without having sex, I was glad cause I really hated it, to me it was something nasty and evil, no matter who it was with.

And when we did have sex I wanted the lights off and my clothes on, I never wanted to get naked, I felt like God would punish me for exposing my body to anyone, my grandmother would tell me that our bodies was the temple for God to live in. But I knew I had to have sex with him to keep him there so we could be a family. So he started leaving a lot, and things got worse for us and I was about 20 years old and was pregnant again, we argue a lot, because I really did not know how to care for two kids and one on the way,

This was not a dream come true, I could not take care of my kids by myself it got hard, I was so scared that I might lose my children because I could not pay rent,

He was not working and that was hard on me, so one day I packed all my clothes and left him and went and stayed with my grandmother, so that she could help me since my uncles were not living there anymore. I felt safe being there. I thought marring this man and having a family with him that this would wipe my angry tears and they would all go away. I thought that this was real true love' the type of love I never had from anyone, but I guess it was not for me. Maybe every foster parent that told me that I would never be loved, I can't get love, and my life was meaningless, maybe that was why my mother gave us away, maybe that's why my grandmother got sick, maybe that's why no one ever cared about me. Now I am 20 years old and I have three children living with my grandmother, as time went on I worked went back to school and was still feeling like my life was empty, how was this?

I have three beautiful children that adore and love me, a grandmother that cared and loved me, she always told me that I was special, and God has a plan for my life that's why I had to go through, she said that I was precious in God eyes and he was going to bless me and use me for his Glory, It was too hard to believe that, why would God want to use a damage vessel like me' for what?

I thought to myself, what is wrong with my grandmother? God don't want me, he hate me he care less what happens to me, and he would never use me with the mess I got in my closet, doesn't he know that I was not pure anymore? And that every man that was a around me took what was precious! So what do I have left to offer God? I am not a virgin any more. So I did what I felt was right for me and my children, I met another guy that was very bad for me, I thought about things that my mother said that between your legs was money so I thought if I would have sex with him and because he was giving me lots of money to care for my kids I was able to buy them anything they ever wanted this man would give me the world as long as I sleep with him,

And this was a nightmare this guy would beat me all the time, my brother was still locked up and could not protect me I had to fight for my life all the time he wanted me to do things I never ever wanted to do so I would fight back, one day he pulled a gun, put it in my mouth because I was going to leave him, he said that he would kill me and my kids, if I ever would leave him, I tried praying but nothing seemed to work, I was too ashamed to tell my grandmother or adopted mother that this was happening so I decided to kill the man myself. I was going to nursing school and had learn a lot about medicine so I plotted to kill him by giving him something in his food, I hated this man he had tried to strip me from the things I loved that was going to college and my kids, so one night he went to sleep and this was the day I plotted to end the pain with him, but he had got a call from his sister so he left the house and his sister boyfriend and him got into something and his sister that she needed him because her boyfriend had jump on her' wow I though you beat woman so why care that he did' but he got up and went over her house and his sister boyfriend shot him instead and he died,

That was my ticket of freedom from him, was it a good way of thinking? I really did not care because I was going to kill him myself, I met another guy that was different he had no kids and seemed to be very nice we dated for awhile, he helped me and my children out a lot, I truly did not know how to treat a man so I would dog him for all the pain I endured in my life, but he stayed and still loved me no Matter what he never hit me or cheated on me, he would just work hard and take care of me and my children like they were his, so we decided to relocated to Duquesne Pa I had some cousins on my father side, and my father sister lived there and they invited me to come live there, so we all moved to better ourselves,

I got back into nursing school, got my kids into church even though I hated it, but I wanted my kids to know that they need to stay with God so that they would not have angry tears like me' I knew mines could never be wiped away.

As time went on I started feeling them feelings that something was still missing in my life, so I would pick fights with the guy I was with making excuses why I did not want him, and he still was good to me no matter what until one day he hit my baby boy and I went off and tried to kill him, no one put their hands on my children not even their own father even though he was never in the picture, but did not play that when it came to my kids,

To get back at him I would met different men that liked me but I hated them, because I knew what they all wanted, and that they all were no good, but I would go out with them to make him mad, until one day he got tired and cheated on me with the baby sitter and I put him out, now I felt more alone when he left and went back to Ohio, so I just dated but would never let them come to my house because I was to scare for them to be around my daughter. I did not trust any men so I treated them like I felt, I dated about 2 different men at this time I was about 23 years old.

I was in college at this time going to school to become a nurse so I could care for my children and they would not need or want anything like I did. I was scared that they would go through what I did. I could not ever lose my children, they were all that I had, and maybe this was all that I would have from God. So I would only thank him for my children, so he would not allow anything to happen to them. Maybe my mother never thanked him for us, maybe this is why her kids were cursed, she had three kids and I had three kids at the time. As time went by me and the guy got backed together and he came back to where I was living, he was the only one besides my kids father I would share everything with, even what was in my past and the things that happened to me. He wanted to marry me but I was still married to my kids father, as time went on I met a friend I worked with me and her was close and her cousin was having a party, a house party and I decided to go with her and my nightmare began again I was date rape, by someone I met at the party' he put something in my drink without my knowledge.

And when I woke up the next day with my clothes off my head was still spinning, but I knew everything that I was seeing, this guy had rape me he was putting on his pants, I started crying and could not believe that this had happened to me again all the way here, I picked up a lamp and hit him on the head, and starting punching him, I was trying to kill this man, his cousin came in the room to pull me off him, and asked what was going on I told him that his friend had raped me.

They started talking in among themselves and I started running toward the kitchen to get a knife, I was going to kill everyone that was in that house, his cousin was telling me to calm down and let's talk, but I was very upset screaming asking him where my girlfriend was? He said she had gone home, I could not believe that she would leave me like this. Did they plan this all along? I thought to myself! Why did she allow them to do this to me? I screamed inside because I had let her know about something's that had happened to me in my past. Was she really a friend? Or did God tell her to pretend she like me so I could be curse again.

Her brother talked to me and took me home saying that he was so sorry for what had happened and he did not know that his cousin had put some type of date rape drug in my soda, but I did not care what he was saying because I was mad inside and was blocking out every word he was saying. When I got home all I could think of is getting even with my so-called friend. I did not care about what I was going to face because I was mad beyond measure, and I could care less about what anyone was going to say. I was to mad at the world again. And now these angry tears were coming back to haunt me. My friend tried to call me but I would not return any of her calls, I was hurt because I believed that she had set me up.

After a while I shook it off, due to I felt like it was my fault' I should of not went their knowing that men were there, and my body did not belong to me.

I was curse to men forever, and I thought that they could take it anytime God said they could, it was that name of the game for me. My relationship will never be the same with any man. How could I explain that I got raped?

I was dressing too sexy for one, and was going out a lot with my friend, no one would believe me anyway, so why bothered.

I was so blown away I knew it was too good to be true living here in another State. Kill me Lord and take me out of my misery, I would say every day, did God make me so that the men would have sex with me? I believe if I did die they would even take it when I am dead, so maybe God should just burn me up. So I put a wall of a hard heart toward all men. Even the man I was with, like it was he fault for letting me go and not protecting me, he never knew why I pushed him away again' so he went back to Ohio, and later I went back to Ohio it was 1983 I had heard that my brother was being released from prison and was looking for me so I had make this the only reason I wanted to come back to a place that only caused me pain and gave me these angry tears,

And me and my male friend got back together and his uncle gave me a house so we moved in together, he knew everything and never judge me no matter what I put him through he was always there for me and my children,

Sometime I would say this is God to me, a man that takes care of you and loves you no matter how many mistakes you make toward him, and he was an awesome father to kids that was not his,

We had a beautiful home and I was everything was going fine. I felt that it was too hard to believe I was living in a fairy tale for anyone to give or do any something this nice without a motive'

But I really did not care my brother had come home again from prison and I wanted him to have a place to come too, and we were s happy to see each other had so much to catch up and for some strange reason I would always bring our real mother up, I always wanted my brother to forgive her like her grandmother would talk to me about forgiveness or we would never be forgiven, so I ask him to go see our real mother so she could know that I had children her grandchildren.

So I asked my brother again and he said yes this time I was so happy, so that weekend was a holiday, Fourth of July he decided to take me to New York I was 24years old.

We started our journey to New York to see our real mother me my brother and his lady friend, we did not know where we was going but we got there I was so scared because my brother still did not like our mother and I was scared of what he would say to her I just wanted us to have a good visit and she would say that she was sorry for what she have done to us and I could tell her about what everyone have done do me and to let her know that I had three children. As we drove through the state of New York it was crazy we seen all types of people, prostitutes, people on drugs it was crazy since they said my mother was a prostitutes so maybe we might see her on the streets. But we found the house someone back home gave us where she lived and we pulled up to the house. And I got out and knocked on the door and a man came to the door and asked me what did I want? I said we were looking for our mother, and he questioned me by asking me what' is your mother name?

And I said her name and he said she lives here, but she doesn't have any kids but one child. And I ask him could she come to the door so we can ask her because the name were the same, and our family told us that our mother lived here. After asking a few times he decided to call her to the door only because he said I look like her so I must be some kin, my stomach started to hurt as he called her to the door, I was scared that she might be another woman, because why don't he know all about her other children? My brother at this time got out the car so that he could hear what was being said, he did not want to see her but wanted to make sure I was okay. She appeared at the door and my eyes were shock because it was her, the same woman that I had lived with, she said what do you kids want?

Like she did not even know us! And I said we came to see you and our little sister, our mother said what little sister? I have only one child, and she is not your sister. I said what? What you are talking about?

Because you are my mother, she said I am not your mother honey, at this time my brother got real upset because we had came so far and this lady was denying that she was our mother. I was so hurt I could not believe she would ever say something like this, she asked us to leave but her male friend wanted to know why we were calling her our mother, so he asked her. And she told him she did not know, she believe we were her sister kids and she help raised us so we might think she was our mother. My eyes were full of angry tears and because I was crying, my brother walked up from his car and was getting real upset because he promised me that no one would ever make me shed a tear again, as long as he was around me and living, so he started telling my mother what he really thought about her and was saying some really bad things, cursing at her, it looked like he was about to hit her, I just wanted them to stop urging, then my mother's male friend came out the door with a big shoot gun telling us to get away from his house,

My brother was not afraid he had walked toward the gun and told him that he had nothing to do with it, our mother was a liar, and we were her kids that she left to die in a house fire when we were just babies,

I was so scared because my brother feared nothing and no one, he told the guy to do what he want to do' shoot because we came to far to let a no good mother like her deny her blood, so shoot me if you think that would solve her mess, but he was going to speak his mind. I started screaming begging my mother to tell the truth so that my brother would not get hurt, but she pushed me away and said that she was going to call the police, so I begged my brother to leave so that he would not get in trouble and he would not go to jail, then his lady friend got out the car and told my brother to get in the car because he could get into trouble. My brother was on parole in Ohio and if they knew that he was in New York he would go back to prison. We only had 20 dollars to our name to get back on, what a hot mess.

And we never got to see our little sister at all I really did not know where she was, if she was in the house or did she get rid of her. I cried all the way back home. I believe my brother now that our mother was no good, she never cared about us and never would, to allow a man to pull a gun on her own son was terrible what kind of mother would let someone take a life of her child? It was a nightmare going to New York, I told my brother that I was sorry and I would never bring her name up again and I was so thankful that God did not allow this man to hurt my brother.

When I got home I told my man friend what my mother had done. It was so hard to put all that behind us. And my brother told me to promise him that if anything ever happened to him that I would not allow that woman to come to his funeral.

I still did not like my brother talking like he was going to die but I promise him that I would not allow her to come because he would not stop talking about it.

Chapter 3

Not My Brother

After time it was about 2 months later my brother ended back in prison they had given him 3 years for violating his probation, and this was hard, but my life went on, me and the man stayed together for a long time and we both had good jobs and nothing bad was happening but I still felt empty and alone with him and my children. Why? Was always my reason to seek to have a relationship with a woman who did not love me, but I continue to worked and took care of home and my friend did to, the 3 years went by fast for my brother to be coming home from prison and he had got paroled to my house, I was so glad we had a lot to talk about, my brother was living with me and another lady friend off and on and every day he was bothering me about getting insurance on him, saying that something might happen to him, my brother always wanting to take care of me no matter where he was, and he did not care a lot about my male friend,

Maybe because he thought that he could not protect me, if something happened to him, my brother did not feel anyone was good enough for his sister, so maybe this is why did I feel that this man could not wipe all my tears away,

Knowing that my brother loved me more than anyone, even God'

Me and my brother caught up on everything he missed in my life, my brother was so full of life and never let nothing or no one stand in his way, at this time I was talking to my brother about forgiving our mother but he still hated her,

I had some nerve when I hated all the people that ever hurt me. And believe me he would get mad at me for even wanting to say her name, but I never gave up on talking to him about her no matter what he said. So time went on and we made the best of living our life the best way we knew how. As time went on my brother would talk to me about getting life insurance on him over and over again,

I would get mad and tell him to stop talking foolish, but he continue saying the same thing over and over I asked him what are you planning to do kill yourself?

I told him don't try, because God would not allow that because I tried to many times to end my life and God would not let me die he wanted us to suffer because we were cursed from having a mother like we did, and her sins infected us from living a normal life, this is what most of the foster homes I lived in told me, my brother told me no, I just want you to be taking care if something ever happen to me. That's why he wanted me to do this. Now it is October 19 of 1984 and this is when my life changed everything that I lived for was really hitting be in the face I could feel everything that ever happened to me come back alive.

I was at work working midnights and a phone call came to my job saying that my brother just got shoot!

I ran from my job jumped in my car and drove straight to the place where my brother was laying in the streets,

With my tears over flowing I jumped out the car and ran toward my brother, I was there before the police and ambulance. Holding my brother in my arms with his head on my lap trying to stop the bleeding and telling him to hold on, saying please don't leave me. my brother was trying to talk but I would not let him, telling him to just hold on I looked up toward a place they say heaven asking God to please don't let my brother die, this is all I have, I know lord that you care less about me and you never answered none of my prayers ever, but would you please have mercy on me and spare my brother's life? My brother was calling my name so I looked down at him and he had one tear coming down his face telling me I love you baby girl, take care of the little soldiers, and he took his last breathe and closed his eyes, as I wiped the tear from my brother eye. I felt nothing, my body was numb,

I don't even know how I made it to the hospital! I was in shock, my bothers best friend was there, and my friend I was working with that night came,

When the doctor came in the room to tell me that they could not save my brother he was gone, I felt my soul leave my body as I collapsed on the floor with no more living in my body, for days I never wanted to talk to God ever again, how my grandmother worshiped this God! Did she know how he was treating her grandchild? I really did not want to let go of my brother no matter what people said or done, I just wanted to be left alone.

Even through my friends had tried to help me deal with this even the man I was with, him and my brother had the same name. But I hated life and everyone around me' but my babies, I held them every night close to me, they tried to wipe my tears away but nothing they did work. Now it is time to prepare for my brother funeral, October 27, 1984, I had to sell things in my house, and people gave money because my brother had no life insurance, I never did what he ask me to do, maybe he knew that he was going to die, maybe God told him that he was going to die?

My mother ha what a laugh came down I really did not want her here, why would she come when she said that we were not here kids? Why did she care? My grandmother always told me to forgive people no matter what they do or say to you. But I did not want to forgive her. I blamed her for my brother getting killed and my brother did not want her here, I had promised him that I would not allow her to come, Maybe the quilt killed her, she should have been ashamed to even showed how face, I said to myself' I had all types of emotion going on inside,

I felt like Sybil, with all types of personalities some time I was up and sometimes I was down, I had wondered how my mother knew that my brother had got killed after she had told her man friend that we were not her children, how did she tell him that she had to come and buried a son after she had told him she only had one child, but I found out that my Grandmother had called to New York and told the man that we were her children,

Because he was her husband now and he had to know the truth, so how does she feel because her little secret was out, the box! The man knew that we were telling the truth' that we were her children.

I wonder how she dealt with that mess. But honestly I did not even care. I was so stressed out and with everybody getting on my nerves like they really cared where was every one when we were going through hell? My mother acted like she had raised my brother all his life with her sad cry. I truly wanted to go with my brother, I asked God so many nights to take me with my brother, but when I looked at my kids I said how could I leave them with these messed up people in this world. No one would take care of them or make sure nothing happened to them. Then I thought about the man I was living with maybe he would care for them, we have been together a long time and he has not tried to mess with my daughter or anything, he loved them like they were his own, he would be the best person I could leave them with, but I was too scared to trust it. And I never want them to feel what I was feeling of losing a love one.

Chapter 4

"Time for a Change

I just could not trust it so I guess I was stuck in this crazy messed up world, maybe God gave me children so I could stay here longer to suffer' but I remember thy shall not kill, my grandmother told me especially taking your own life,

But I wanted to kill my mother, father, uncle, and all them foster home parents, especially the guy that took my brother away. I felt that everyone who allowed things to happen to me, were not innocent by no means.

But times got so hard for me to deal with, I did not want to go to work, go outside or out my room, ever since my brother was murdered, it has been six months, I was not doing good at all so we decided to move to Utah a family member asked me to come they felt it might help to leave Ohio, so I went first to get things together for my family and a cousin had invited me to stay with him and his wife so I could get my life back in order and better myself there, him and his wife would help me out, so I decided to move to Utah so I could finish Nursing, I had an 1& 1/2 half year to go.

My male friend wanted to go but he had a job and was coming up later after I find a place for us to stay, so I went while he and the kids stayed just for three months.

I Was in Utah for 30 days got a job and a place to live because I had to work fast while I was staying with my cousin and his wife, I was very uncomfortable his wife was very nice, but he was nuts he looked at me all the time when I walked, he made me feel so uncomfortable, and wanted to hug too much and then one night he tried to have sex with me, I was doing so well and things looked great until my own blood relations started making sexual movements on me. I really thought that God would not allow this to keep going on' maybe it was out of his control! I started thinking that I had a tattoo on me that only the world could see and not me saying body for anyone to touch, I hated my body, I looked at it like it was nothing but evil,

I pulled a knife on him and he told me to get out his house, his wife was scared of him, but she believed me and tried to help me, so she gave me money to get a motel room for a week I was so mad and upset.

Here I was again, that I would come over two thousand miles from Ohio and the same plague in my family has followed me again! I guess I was cursed and nothing and nowhere would make a difference at all. I worked hard to get my place I had a nice job and met some good friends that helped me out better than people in Ohio.

I wanted God to allow me to rest and never wake up, I thought relocating to Utah would be better and help some of my angry tears. Maybe a change of scenery would help me; it was hard to be in Ohio where my brother lost his life.

I found a place that was so nice and my male friend and children came up he had got a job on the Air Force Base, I was too ashamed to tell him what really happened,. I knew God was punishing me. I would ask myself all the time why did God make me a pincushion?

At this time my boys were getting older they knew my friend was not their real father but I did not allow them to go back to Ohio to see their father because he was not trying to do anything in his life at that time, and I wanted more for my sons, and he never asked, all I ever wanted was to better myself and do better by my children, better then my parents were with me.

When I lost my brother I just could not face life at that time. I wanted to thank him but my heart was to numb and heavy to open my mouth to say the words. He had brought my family together, I never had anything to be thankful for only my children, and I thank the Lord for that.

So as time went on I started messing up the relationship with the man I was with, I did not know how to love, I did not believe in love, and I was scared to even receive love, because I thought it would be only a joke played on me! So I kept my heart hard.

All I ever wanted was my children to be happy, and my kids loved it in Utah, my male friend and I had good jobs. We were doing well. But still I was hurting for something that was still missing in my life. What is it I wonder to myself?

I have a nice home, a nice car, a good job, good friends, a good man, awesome children, and nice clothes and shoes, I had enough stuff to give to 20 families. I had love from lots of people now that I never knew that could love someone like me, so what was missing out of my life? So I hid everything that ever happened to me inside, I cried off and on, no one could understand what was going on with me, I was an emotional roller coaster. Even though I had a good man at home I wanted more maybe that was what it was, so I dated other men even though I did not care much for them I just wanted to use them I wanted to hurt every man the way I was hurt.

So I only use them for what I could get out of them but that still did not fill the emptiness that was stabbing me in the heart.

Because every man I came into contact with always wanted sex for love, it was always drop the pants or pull up your skirt, what do this got to do with love? Even sex did not wipe my tears away. I was so closed up inside full of hurt, shame and pain. I felt that this was a way of life for everyone maybe other people went through the same thing I went through and just kept it inside, maybe they moved to new places so no one could identify them.

It was nice to be somewhere where other people did not know what happened to you, so I separate myself from family and made up family as I met new people, I did not like my real family at all I thought they had some type of disease that allowed them to act the way they did and I did not want my children to inherit that disease, so I kept them away. I stayed in Utah for 8 more years and my baby sister had got older and had got in touch with me what a good thing.

So I sent for her to come and live with us in Utah she had a male friend and I did not care I just wanted her with me so we could wipe each other's tears away, but when she came I was disappointed she came with a house full her man his brother and his lady friend I did not know these men and did not trust them around my children at all, they looked rough and my sister did too at this time, I just wanted to help her, We talked laugh and cried together she had told me all kinds of things that had happened to her I hated the mother we called mom for how she raised my sister rough, my sister never had a good normal life a life of drugs, prostitution, sex, and crime, what a life to have as a childhood.

No wonder she had a choice of bad men in her life my heart hurt for her, but after a while I could not keep them their because of all the fighting that was going on between them and the other couple and my friend said they had to go so after a real bad fight one night I had to let them go, but me and my baby sister stayed in touch no matter what.

Her life was full of in and out of prisons just like my brother, I was upset with my man friend because I hated to choose to send my sister away because she got into trouble and I were not able to help wipe her tears away.

So we had problems one after another but he still was excellent to my children, as time went on it was 1990 I started to get sick and I stayed sick all the time, I could not understand what was going on so I went to the doctors and took all kinds of test I was not pregnant and that was good, but something worst was going on they told me that I had cancer I just could not believe my ears what a trauma, I can't have this no I said to myself why is everything always happening to me! Doesn't God have someone else to pick on? I can't have cancer who is going to care for my children who? I started really not liking this God but still was too scared to stop my kids from serving him, because he took care of them nothing happened to them like it happened to me, so I kept them in church more and more,

I talked to one of my friends about my sickness and she was crying with me and she told me about a hospital that helped her aunt but the hospital was in New York I have not thought of that place no more since my brother died that was the place my Real mother lived' what was God trying to do to me, I really wanted to go to New York so I could get well and get rid of this cancer so that I could live and care for my children myself, so as time went by I got sicker and weaker and could not care for myself I spent most of my time in bed, and my Grandmother called and told my mother that she need to help me since she never done anything for me in the past.

So she did contact me and told me that Rochester had the best cancer hospital called Strong Memorial Cancer hospital and she wanted me to come there.

She came down met my male friend and her grandchildren again the last time she meet them was in 1985 when my brother Curtis had passed away.

And she helped me drive back east because I was to week to drive, my male friend stayed because we had too much stuff to get together to move for me, and he had to wait to come later so he could get things together, we talked a little on the way to New York not much, I really did not have much to say I was to mad at God to even had put me in this situation. We arrive at the hospital in New York it was very big, I really did not want to stay because I had to let my mother care for my children, I did not trust her by any means necessary, but what choice did I have. But I did threaten her and let her know that nothing better not happen to my kids while they were in her care or I would blow New York up with her and her husband in it. She looked at me like I was crazy, and I said to myself I am crazy when it comes to my children, so I wrote a will just in case anything happened to me in the hospital I wanted my kids to go back with my male friend or my auntie in Ohio.

I was In the hospital getting well it had been six months I was going for chemo and radiation treatment my male friend had drove up and got a place for us.

That was good because I did not want to be around a woman that really did not love me, and I thought that the reason why she stepped in to help is that if I die she would get my kids and money and everything I ever owned.

After being there eight month the doctors could not find any kind of cancer in my body like it was never there, they ran all kinds of test over and over again and nothing, what a joke everyone told me that it was God and my grandmother said that it was one of God miracles, I did not believe that because I knew that God hated me so why would he heal someone like me? Nevertheless I stayed in New York I got a job at the hospital and my man friend was working, even though I was cured from cancer I still felt that I was dead inside, something was eating inside of me I still did not feel the love I needed to wipe my angry tears away. I was in a very rebellious state of mind, I did not care or love anyone but my children, so I completely mess up my relationship with my man friend I was with for thirteen years, the love he was trying to give me was not enough to heal me from the pain that had me shed so many angry tears,

I was tired of living with him sleeping with him or looking at him, I never wanted to marry him because I was still married to my sons father we never divorced, the relationship I had built with my mother was not good enough because all we did was argued because she felt that she never done anything wrong living her life as a one big lie after another.

At this time I had heard that my father was sick living with my aunt in Detroit I had not forgiven my father for what he had done to me, even though he was in my life off and on, when I was living in Ohio he knew my children better than my mom because he tried to make up with me over and over again, it was that my pain was so deep it was too hard to let him in.

My father was still drinking and I was scared to let him too close to me so I monitor him with my children when he was in their life, it was so funny because my father was so good with my children and they loved their grandfather, I never told them anything bad about him, I wanted them to have a relationship with him in spite of what he did to me.

I loved my father because he really had tried to be a good father. He tried to buy me everything I ever wanted. But it never made up enough to wipe my angry tears away. I got a call that my father had died January 1991.

I cried it really hurt that I was not able to forgive him I really loved my father and it was too late to let him know that, I went to the funeral me and my man friend, and when I actually seen him laying in the casket I broke it hurt so much to see him laying there I beg him to forgive me for not forgiving him, I told him that I loved him even though he did not hear me I really felt that he heard me,

I cried out loud and said daddy I love you forgive me for how I ever treated you' I just never had told him that because my hurt and pain would not let me forgive him.

While I was at my father funeral, I meet two sisters & a brother that my father had while he was living in Chicago there were younger than me we talked a little I really did not know them at all, I never knew that my father had other children,

I was to hurt to really cared all I knew is that I was his only child. But I always wanted a family and this is when I found out I had a brother and two sisters that I met it blew my mind because I always believed my father only had me.

After the funeral I went back to New York my mother act like she did not care that my father even died, she would tell me I never want to hear that name in my house, that because she had lied to her husband about my father he never knew that she was married to my father before, he only knew about my sister father. She was a hot mess because I was proud of my father no matter what he had done in the past,

I only wanted to remember that he really loved me. He was a professional boxer but his drinking destroyed his life. After a while things got bad in my relationship and I did not want to be with my man friend, So we split up, at this time I did not care about my life I thought if I would be happy it was a sin, or something and God would punish me for it, so why try.

I could not stand my mother's husband he was very sneaky, every time he see me he looked just like the foster parents men look at me like I was something to eat, I did not like the way he touched me or talk to me my mother was in such a denial concerning him that man was no good and up to no good.

But he never tried to mess with me he knew I would cut him up in sizes, I had always asked my daughter did he ever tried to touch her or make her feel uncomfortable and she said no, so he was lucky.

So I moved back to Ohio and started back with the life I had, Now it is September 1991 my baby brother had lost his life, just a baby I just could not receive this another brother I had to see leave my life, I loved my baby brother so much no one would of thought I was his adopted sister because we were so close and his smile had always light up a room he murdered just like my older brother from gunshots wounds,

I really could not deal with the bad news it was so bad that other young men died with him, how much more pain will I shed tears about?

I never knew that a person could shed that many tears, as times went on, I wanted to move it seemed like Ohio was bad for me, but in 1994 my Adopted mother was very ill she had cancer, I really did not want to move away and not be there for her, but all the bad memories here in Ohio, but I had to stay and help care for her after all she had done for me, she had saved me from all the monster in that place,

I wished she would of known about all the monster's all over because she would of made sure that I was protected, I hated to move back to a place where nothing but punishment was at. But if I had to go through anything then it will not matter because what could get worst then what I have already been through?

So I packed up my children they were much older to care for themselves so I put them in a home and I stayed at my adopted moms home a lot to care for her for awhile,

Chapter 5

"My Life Really

Things were getting rough at this time because of me quitting my job to care for a woman that loved me more than my own mother and I felt like I was getting ill again myself, and my cancer had came back and I did not want anyone to know, because we were going through enough with my adopted mom, so I had applied for disability so I could get help and was waiting on that to come through so times were rough like always in the this place, I was going to the club sometimes with family members and meeting all the wrong people but I really did not care at the time it was six months later and I still had not received any income and I was losing my home,

So a guy that I was dating asked me to move in with him at this time I was going to church with a foster sister of mine and they taught us that we do not live with men unless we are married to them or the wrath of God would come down on us, that was a joke because the wrath of God was already on my life, I had no choice,

So it was killing me to do this and I hated it because I never wanted to live with this guy or any guy, he was not my kind of man at all but he gave us a roof over my head and food on the table for me and my kids, none of my family helped me out so this is what I had better than being homeless.

and my life was fading in front of me this man did everything I hated in a man sex, drugs, he was a male prostitute and I was dealing with trying to live for God, a friend I met invited to his church and for once in my life, I decided to give my life to God I heard one day that if you be born again you would be a new creature, and God will wipe all your tears away, that stuck with me and I wanted to be born again so I could have a new identity then maybe God would bless me like he did the people in the church.

So times got worse and things got touch, I went to church one night and the preacher was preaching about if you live in sin you would go to hell and I was scared that I had my kids living in sin and I did not want them to go to hell and then I heard the message concerning a family in the bible,

How what he did cursed his children and I felt like that was what my mother had did to me and my brother cursed our life so I decided to take my own life so that my kids would not suffer from my mistakes like my mother did me, Then I heard a message that if you do not forgive then God would not forgive you and I could not forgive my mother or my uncles nor my foster parents or my kids father why should I? they do not deserve my forgiveness they had messed up my life, this is why I am like I am, I wanted to be a virgin until I got married, I wanted to be married before I had any children, I only wanted one man in my life, I wanted to obey the ten commandments but how could I? They made it impossible for me to do this. Life was not fair at all for me I was domed, I could not take it anymore, the man I was with was a dog he slept with everyone that he could had a baby on the way and it seemed like God would not bless me to move for nothing in the world it was not what I wanted for my children.

The house was not what we was use to living in, and I hated this for my kids it looked like all the foster homes I lived in a hot mess, drinking, cursing, just a wild life I had took out a nice insurance policy on myself and asked the man that had helped me raise my kids that I was with for 13 years would he raise them if anything ever happened to me and he said he would, we talk all the time because we were still good friends. So it was New Years Eve I thought about taking my life so that my kids would have a good life with the large insurance policy I had, they would be well off and get out this rat hole of a place, but when I tried I was reading the policy and writing my kids a letter and trying to take the pills but whatever it was made me sick and my asthma kicked in the large pill got stuck in my throat and I could not get it out it had blocked my lung where I could not breathe at all no one was around to help me. I was praying that no would think I tried to commit suicide because the insurance policy would not pay. So I was not trying to kill myself, I wanted to but it would have been worst for my children,

I was trying to take my asthma pill when it got stuck down the wrong pipe and the next thing I knew I was in a coma and woke up march 12 1995 three months had went by and I never knew I was in a coma but I heard voices through it all, I knew that people were talking to me, and I could not answer them,

I had lost oxygen to my brain for over 12 hours before anyone found me lying on the floor next to the couch unconscious on top of my 2-year-old granddaughter.

My daughter had a baby girl, and I named her Shekinah that I loved dearly, God had given me the name before she was born, a ministry the lord spoke in me, but because I was not living right at the time to start any type of ministry when I needed it myself, I put the name on my first born grandchild.

The whole time I was in the coma, my deceased brother was talking to me, I could see him and hear him telling me to go back, I could not come with him my children need me and I got a great life ahead of me, he kept saying that I had life's depending on me, that God was going to use me!

And then he said follow me toward the light and I followed him he gave me a hug and told me that he loved me and he was with me and will always be with me. And then I woke up from being in the coma, it was three months later every nurse and doctors came in my hospital room and called me a miracle child they had already had diagnosed me as being brain dead or a vegetable and told my children and family to prepare to buried me, I was living on life support for three months. I had remembered almost everything, my kids, my name, half my family and everything that I had owned. What did God want with me? Why was he saving me every time I try to die? What is my purpose here on earth? What does he have in me that need to live? I had so many questions in my head for God.

Everyone was so happy to see me awake, I had got all types of visits from people I never knew church People, business people, professional people, why do people care? I asked myself over and over again.

As time went by it seemed like nothing ever had happen I was walking and talking and doing the things I use to do,

Everyone was shock to see how I recovered so soon, when the doctor's said that I would not make it and if I had I would be brain dead or a vegetable, I was in a coma for three months and came home in a wheel chair but was walking by the time my daughter graduated. It was within three months and I was back to my routine again. Every church person I talked with said God got something great for you to do, his angel was protecting me and his grace and mercy was over my life, I thought about that and I wanted to believe that but it was too hard to receive, thinking about what had happened in my past. At this time I was going to church but was not saved. I was going because a man friend of my brother had invited me, he had told me that my brother had told him to look after me, my brother it was hard to believe because my brother was not a church boy so how did he hang with this guy but I found out later that my brother was friends with his brother and they knew each other, so I starting going to church with him I was still living with the guy I was with before I was in a coma,

I remembered this day good this day changed my life it was my birthday September 1, 1996 I walked in the church the doors seemed to open all by themselves, I felt like I was someone very important because everyone came up to me and shock my hand they seemed to be very nice, then the pastor and his wife came up and his wife gave me a big hug and said in my ear God told me that you would be coming soon, I looked surprise because I did not know her but she seemed to know me and she told me her and her husband had came to visit me in the hospital, and had prayed for me every day and knew God had too much work for me to do,

I felt very welcome the songs and testimonies and the preaching word was awesome, as I sat in my seat I kept hearing a soft voice talking to me, I thought it was my friend talking to me, but when I looked at him his mouth was not moving he was praising God, then I heard the voice again saying come to me and I will give you rest and wipe them tears away! And love you like no other can, the voice was so strong that it moved my whole body.

I never felt this way before, I jumped up and my legs started trembling and I started to shake and tears were flowing down my face, like a river. I could not stop myself the closer I got to the alter I started feeling lighter and lighter, I felt like I never felt before, I could not understand what was happening all I knew is that it felt good, a feeling I never felt in my life.

I finally was at the altar and the pastor came to me and asked me did I want to be saved? Give my life to Jesus? I did not understand, I thought he wanted me to hang on the cross like Jesus did for us, he gave his life for us, so I thought I had to do the same thing, so the pastor explained what being save meant, by letting me know that I had to be Godly sorry for all my sins, and ask God to forgive me for all the sins I have done, except God to come in my heart, allow the lord spirit to live in me, believe in my heart that Jesus died for my sins, be baptize in Jesus name so that I could be cleanse with the blood of Jesus, and allow the lord to renew my mind by reading his word daily,

Believe that Jesus is my lord and savior, I could not stop the tears from coming down my face it was like we needed a bucket, all I ever wanted was God to love me and wipe all my angry tears away.

So I screamed yes' I had excepted what the pastor was saying, I did not understand why I had to repent and say I was sorry for anything or to ask for forgiveness, because I felt everything I have done up to this point was not my fault, and why the people that made me this way' why they did not have to repent and ask for forgiveness?

But at that moment a voice let me know that the things that happen had to happen for a great purpose in my life and I would understand as I walk with him daily, I was so shock that God was really talking to me, the first time ever I heard his voice speaking to me and answering my questions. Maybe the lord do care for me, what have I done to deserve this I wondered? I screamed loud saying Lord please forgive me, please save me, I am so tired lord of living the way I have been living,

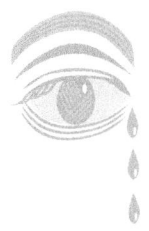

Chapter 6

'Make Me New Lord!

Lord I am tired of feeling the pain and sorrow I have been feeling lord, I am tired please come into my life and fix it lord, make me a new person lord, a better person lord, please forgive me for all my sins and forgive the ones that sinned against me,

I forgive them lord, please forgive me, make me over, I want to be born again. Lord wipe all the angry tears that I have shed, I want a change lord, I believe you died on the cross for me, lord help me, please help me, I surrender my all to you, I cast every heavy load I got and every angry tear I shed at your feet.

I realize at that moment I was truly tired of being tired of the way I was living, I felled to my knees on the floor at the altar, at that moment I received feeling that had took control of me I started shouting the name of the lord, Jesus Jesus, Jesus, is all my mouth was moving saying, and I had no control of it my body was feeling great, I was feeling like I never felt before, I felt so good, I never wanted to stop, I felt the heaviness of my heart being lifted off of me, and my tears were not tears of sorrow or pain but joy and happiness,

I danced all over that church no one could hold me it was too powerful. They could not baptize me until the following Sunday because I praised the lord all that day. When I got home things felt different I looked at myself for the very first time in a mirror and saw nothing but beauty, I was looking good, I looked like a bright shining star,

I did not see that little girl that was ugly, scared, unwanted, abandon, rejected, abused or ashamed. I wanted to live, and start living this new life I was giving again. I had read in the bible that you can cast all you cares and all your past sins on God and he would cast it in the sea of forgetfulness and you can start over and your tomorrow is brand new,

So it was time to make some changes in my new life, I could not live with this guy I was living with, but I had no money still waiting on my disability to come, so I also read in the bible that if your life be pleasing to God you can ask what you need and God would supply all your needs according to his riches and glory, and I need to please God so my life could be pleasing in his eyes.

I really did not know how to pray and I heard my friend say just talk to God like you would your man friend or kids or just talk to him like he was your best friend, so I got in a secret place of the house and purred out my heart out to God and told him what I needed to be able to start living right for him, and boy didn't prayer work they next two days my disabilities check came before the approval letter,

It was enough to get a house, buy furniture, a car, and food for me and my kids, I moved in 12 hours thanking God for all he was doing for me I never took care of myself by myself it was always someone I had to depend on like a man, but this time God was my new man now and I did not haven't to sleep with the lord to be bless, all he ever wanted from me was a relationship, as I was reading my bible daily and going to church I found out that God was a jealous God and would not have any other Gods before him. The way I was feeling lately it was like I was born for the very first time. It felt like I was loved for the very first time in my life, everything was going great,

I loved waking up starting my day, going to church and praising God, I still wanted to know why I had to forgive those who really cared less about me, so I was learning about having a hard heart, bible study was on having a clean heart, it seemed like every time I would enter into the house of God It was teaching me something new I thought that I was okay because I gave my life and excepted Christ in my life, but I never knew I had to learn how to overcome the past that had me still bond.

My mind had to be renewed, and my heart had to be created new, and the right spirit had to be dwelled inside of, and my flesh had to die daily, I still had hatred in my heart for my mother for giving me away, I had blamed her for everything that ever happened to me, and I still have no forgiveness toward my uncles and foster parents and any man that ever hurt me, I had a murderous heart, because I wanted to kill the man that killed my brother, I had a fornication heart because of the man I had slept with still,

I had a rebellious heart because I still wanted to get even with people that ever hurt me, I had a jealous and envy heart because I hated and wanted what other families had with their children, and I had a deceitful heart because I still had the secret of who my daughter father was, I never knew that all these things was hindering me from God true blessings on my life, so now I am taking baby steps all over again learning how to become me. A person God created.

I had a shameful heart because I was ashamed of anyone knowing what happened in my past, I had an unclean heart because of all the evil things I had hid inside, I had to learn how to love and forgive myself first, then I could feel my heart being made new, when this started happening then I saw a new child of Christ being made over, and what a beautiful person I started to become, it seemed like I was a total different person in the same body.

Everywhere I went and everything I touched was bless, I started to call my mother every mother's day and her birthday and holidays letting her know how me and her grandkids were doing, our relationship was not totally whole yet.

But I was working on a relationship with her and God was giving me the strength to over look some of her ways, I was not scared to be in a room with older men, I wanted to help and share my story with foster kids and lost teens that have been abused or anyone that God sent my way, I was proud to share my testimony with others. I had to let them know that God will wipe their tears away if they give them to him, And let them know that with Jesus all things are possible and God can change their night into day, I wanted everyone that ever been through some or half or either of the things I been through, and to let them know that the lord will and has heard their cry and they do not haven't to be ashamed of anything that was out of their control, but God will and can turn it around for his glory, I wanted to tell the world how God turned my sorrow into joy, my mid-night into day and to never give up on what God can do. Every time I tell my story I thought about that light I had seen while I was in the coma and to tell you the truth I know now that it was God who had sent an angel dressed as my brother,

When God need to get your attention he would use anything or anyone to let you know that you are his chosen, thank you Jesus I could not believe that I could open my mouth up every day to say thank you lord, something that was blocked in me was now opened, when I truly looked back on my life thinking about what I had to do just to feed my children,

I almost ended up in prison by hanging with people that really did not care about my destiny, I had allow myself to do things that I hated doing, committing fraud with my mother allowing her to mess my life up, just like she had help my sister do.

But through the grace of God I have been given another chance to do this right, now the time has come, 1996 my adopter mother had turn for the worst her cancer had got so bad, I was so sad to see her suffer the way she did, I prayed so many days and night that God would ease her pain, I would sit with her and talk with her, she would always let me know that she was so proud of me.

I never had anyone tell me that they were proud of me, these few words meant a lot to me because she had never told me, and I did not know if I truly mattered but her words were so heartfelt, and the next day I was sitting there giving here morphine mediation because she was in so much pain I prayed that God please help her. By taking her home or cure her, and at that moment she past, I was so hurt but was glad that she did not haven't to suffer no more.

After two years of battling lung cancer my adopted mom past away, At the last hour I had with my adopted mother I had read the bible to her and prayed with her to let her know to give her life to God at that last hour that she had even though I did not know that she was going in that hour, But I know that she ask God to forgive her for all her sins and that she know that Jesus died for her sins, and she invited him in her heart, and that had gave me peace.

I never felt that my adopted sisters and brothers were nothing but my real family, that is how close we were, but when my adopted mom past we kind of drifted apart,

At this time I was living pay check to pay check even though I had the lord on my side and I was in church I kind of meet another man he was in the church so I really thought it was okay to date and I just knew he was different than the men I have dated in my past, that was the worldly men and this was a spiritual man, lord wasn't I blind to the fact that a man is a man, if he don't allow God to be in control of his flesh, well it was this one night I decided to go over his house to watch a Christian movie with him he had invited me over I did not feel that it would be wrong to do, since he said he had invited others from the church, but I was feeling a feeling not to go, but I thought he is a man of God, what could happen? If only I knew, if only I listen to the voice that was saying no inside.

Lord what is going on? I said to myself, well he had given me a cold drink he said he make all the time for the Pastor and no one had came over yet, his phone ring and he said it was the rest saying that they could not make it, I started to feel dizzy and felt him touching me,

I just could not believe what was happening to me a Godly man forced his self on me telling me that I am going to marry you so don't worry, I tried to push him off me but he was to strong it felt like it was de'javu, lord where did I go wrong?

This man' a man of God had just raped me. What and who can I talk to? Who would believe me? And he felt like there was nothing wrong, like it was okay because he was a man of God or what!

I did not go to church for two weeks, and the people of the church kept calling me and because I would not answer they started coming by, but I just told them I just was sick with the flu, after a while I did confine in a sister at the church and she told the pastor, so the pastor wanted to have a meeting with me and the brother in the church, so we did and the results was that the pastor had quote a scripture in the bible In Matthew saying that we cannot take our brethren to the law of the land, that we haven't to reason together in the church,

I was so confuse and could not believe that you can rape someone in the church and just have a meeting in this meeting he also quote another scripture 1 Corinthians chapter 7 and that it was better to marry than to burn, it was so hard for me to hold back the tears that were in my heart, I could not believe that they wanted me to marry a man that I did not love and did not know, but I did like him at the beginning, even through what he did was not right all he had to do is confess that he did it and ask for forgiveness and that was all, I really did not know a lot about the word at this time so whatever they told me I believed, I just did not want the lord to turn his back on me again, so whatever I had to do to keep the lord on my side I obeyed the man that had rule over my life another word he would quote to me from Hebrews

13-17 he convince us that we should get married because the brother was about to be a minister and they needed him to have a wife before he could be. What a joke and my friend I trusted the sister at the church who was supposed to have my back agreed with what was going on.

Chapter 7

"Marry Him or Hell

And the program went on I did what I thought I had to do to make it into the kingdom of God, I did what I thought I had to do for God to be proud of me and to love me, all I wanted was to be save and make it to heaven, me and my children.

So I married this man, a man the church had choose for me not the one God had for me, the funny thing was we got married on a bible study night, but the pastor did not want us to let anyone know that we were married, I never understood that at all, it was a couple of months before we had the real ceremony, and this is when we were allowed for people and the saints to know, even though I felt like I made the biggest mistake of my life, all I felt was I was not lonely anymore and all I got from him was lust and rejection, I was just happy to know that God was please that I was with my own husband and not a man that was not, so I just settle with what I had, but still unhappy. So as time went by I enjoyed working in the church I song in the choir, worked being a usher, help clean the church,

Did tape ministry, and minister to people by being a soul winner for the lord, I read my word daily, I fast and prayed and talk to God all the time, but to tell you the truth I was still hurting inside, I really did not feel loved by this man, I only felt like it was a duty, he would give me a allowance weekly only what the pastor would tell him to give me, fifty dollars, I felt like I was a slave cooked, clean and have sex that's all it was sex not love only a duty to do as his wife it felt like he was using the bathroom on me because I felt numb all the time' I hated it.

I asked God to help me love this man, because he was my husband by law. But as time pass by I was getting weary, all he would do is work come home eat and ask me to read the bible for him and give him my notes so he could use them when he preached, where was I at in this make believe marriage? So I started getting restless and started making mistakes and he would tell the pastor everything even our sex life, well I started reading the word for myself and asking God for wisdom and knowledge and his understanding in his word for me,

I just got tired of them telling me what the word meant, what God was saying concerning my life instead of them telling me that the women duty was to be a help met for her husband and silence in church, So I started asking questions, and I was told that I was acting rebellious, because I did not agree with some things that they would say, at this time I was helping a lot of children and children with handicaps, so I had took in a young lady that was mentally challenge, and she was going to church with me at this time the pastor wanted to see her in the office and she did not feel comfortable with him alone, so she had ask me to sit in some of their sessions, so I let him know that if he wanted to talk to her then I need to be present with her, since I was her guardian, And he told me no, so I would not let him talk with her alone, so I got put out the church and was told that they were taking me to court for false statement that I claimed against the pastor, because I refuse to let him talk with her alone, what kind of church that would kick you out for a mistake? That they accused you of,

All because I call the police to tell them what happened to me and I believe they were going to do the same to the young lady, and since I did and wanted to ask for forgiveness then I was dome, I really was hurt, everyone in the church had turned their backs on me,

The church members were not allowed to talk with me or pray for me, and to top it off, they had the husband they gave me the man I was sleeping with turn his back on me, he would separate himself from me, which was fine with me because I really hated sleeping with him and being his slave just by marriage, it had got so bad because I had been through a lot at this time, while I was married to this man, my body had got afflicted, I had became very ill my lungs had collapsed and I had to be on twenty four hour oxygen, due to stress, and not knowing if someone was doing something to me or not, because my test I would get had some type of drugs in my system that I was not taking at all.

And I had develop stenosis of the spinal and it would paralysis me from the waist down, I ended up in a wheel chair for six months and had to use oxygen for one year, and believe me, I could not understand what in the world I did, but it had to be something that the Lord would be mad at me again, this is what I was taught in the church that if something bad happen to you while you were walking with God, then you had to do something wrong to deserve it, I never knew that when a person fall short, that the church would turn their back on you and kick you out of the place you need to get help from and to tell people not to pray for you, I thought that I was in a make believe movie. But I knew that It was real after three years of long suffering I was healed from being in a wheel chair and I was healed from being on the oxygen and the marriage was falling apart, I was not his dream robot wife he wanted, shut up and put out, and obey. I really did not care about making this marriage work because I was in a mental, controlling relationship,

I was not allowed to think for myself or read the word and understand the wisdom and knowledge God was giving me.

I felt like my past was repeating itself and I was getting discourage with no one to talk to, but the people that was of the world. So I found myself slipping back into my old self, at this time my faith in God had decrease instead of increase.

So I found myself falling and not knowing how to get back up, I had a cousin I loved so much who has always had my back, who came over to check on me, ready to blow the church up and clip and stick the pastor, and the man I was married to he tried to make me feel good but you see even though I was saved by grace I felt Like I was out of place, I did not feel the love from God anymore, I knew that God had wiped my angry tears away from the past, but what about the future ones?

I went backwards instead of forward, I was too scared to ask God for forgiveness because of how I was treated by his people I felt that God was the same way, and plus I had messed up so bad that my shame had came back to haunt me.

In 2002 I received my divorce, boy I felt just like a failure I had a marriage in the world and it did not work' now I am married in the church and it still did not work. I just was so upset with my life I ran from God instead of asking him for his help. I wanted to go back to God but I was to scare of God's rejection. I listen to friends & family and even my enemies to mess up my life more, even when I tried to do good it seemed like evil was always present,

I tried to live my life like I use to but I felt a stranger living in a different body a feeling came over me, I could not get any rest, my heart was very troubled so one night I went to a club with my favorite cousin, but after twenty minutes of being there a voice kept telling me I did not belong here, and that God see and hears all my angry tears, so I end up leaving and going home.

I started crying asking God what do you want from me? When I arrived home I sat at my bedside and looked at the bible I had on my bed, I felt if I kept the bible in my bed no man would enter,

As I picked up the bible I drop it and the bible had open up to Psalms 34 verse 18 and 19 Saying the lord is nigh unto them that are of a broken heart and saves such as have a contrite spirit, many are the affliction of the righteous, but the lord delivered him out of them all. And then the lord spoke to me in Psalms 147 verse 3 saying he heal the broken in heart and bind up their wounds, but why should I so I had relied on these words? When every day of my life was full of shame & blame, and found myself asking God again to forgive me, I repented of my sins once again I thought that God would be tired of me by now, Using him as a revolving door, in and out, at this time I was to empty my life was over and it was time to leave this messed up place my kids were grown on their own and I was just too tired to fight, the enemy had made me feel like a failure because being divorce twice was not acceptable in the church, and then came my shame again feeling I had set a bad example for my children and the people I were had minister too,

I was feeling myself abandoned and rejected so here I go again maybe I thought to myself that I was only suppose to go to a certain point of my life and then that was it. Was I ever going to find true happiness? Did God love me they way he love others I wondered,

Or did he just plug his ears to my cry? I allowed myself to go in a place that was darker than I ever could imagine, I shut down all together if God would not kill me, than I would never eat! Then maybe I would starve to death! Since cancer could not kill me, a coma could not kill me, me not walking could not kill me, my lungs could not kill me, Me being raped, molested, rejected, abandoned, being in a domestic violence relationship, shamed, could not destroy me, then maybe if I just fade away God would let me go. I just did not care anymore; I turned my back on the word of God and everything that had to do with God. I was so angry and mad that I shut my heart down to feel, sometimes I felt like God word was just a big lie? I just did not care.

I went back to the life I was use too, a life of pain. After losing a so many people I loved I felt like God was punishing me.

But I had read in the word that God cannot be mark, there is nothing under the sun that God don't know he is an all knowing and all seeing God, I never wanted to live because if I tried to live life was going to let me down, no matter what. I was just a laughing vessel for entertainment. Was there really love for me? Was there ever going to be someone like my brother who loved me through it all?

At this point I really did not care before I left the states I had slipped back into a backsliding position, I was going out again and living like I never knew God, but something in me made me feel convicted, I felt strange, like I was in a place I never knew. I felt like I was heading for danger, but I really did not care, I remembered the night I went out with my cousin and this stranger asked me what was I doing in a place like this because I don't seem like the type that hangs out in clubs?

And at this point of my life I really did not care I answered him by saying looks are deceiving, we talked for a while and just before he walked away he said to me don't allow your identity be what the world haven't to offer, and know that there is one person that really cares about them angry tears! I was stunned because how did he know about my tears? Who was this guy? I never meet him before, when I turned around to see where he went I could not find him, I walked around the club at least a dozen times and he was nowhere to be found, after hating myself and mad at the world and wanting to harm myself, my son in Germany sent for me to come there for a while to spend the holidays with his family and to get away from things and to clear my head. So I went to Germany for about two months to get away from people, places and things, but did I really?

Even though it was so nice to get away, my problems followed me, I woke up feeling the same way I felt at home, and I was in a different country trying to run from God, and here he was, here. I had wondered to myself where did I go wrong, I thought I was serving God with all my heart mind and soul,

I was giving him all that I had in me trying to live right, praying, fasting, going to church, doing everything I was told to do, where did I go wrong? Here I am a failure in my walk with God, I can't even serve God! Right, I said to myself, I have failed my kids, and God.

So it was time to leave Germany I had a good time and enjoyed being with my grandkids and daughter-in-law and my son, it was great, but my tears were still heavy and still there. And I never told them what I really was dealing with, My mind was still in a state of confusing, I had grew to love this God and I feared his word and did not understand why I had to go through so much in my life.

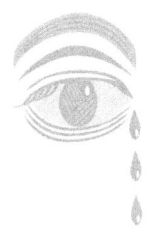

Chapter 8

"I Rather Die!

Now it is 2005 a new year again I was back home I just arrived I unpacked my suitcases and the doorbell rang and it was a sister from the old church I first gave my life to God, the church that hurt me deeply, I wondered what did she want I loved her a lot we were like sisters, she was my foster sister at a time and I loved her two daughters, she asked me how was I doing and I let her know that I just got back from Germany visiting my baby boy and his family, and she gave me a hug and said that she loved me and was praying for me,

I looked shocked because the church we were at together did not want them to talk with me or pray for me, they felt that I was a lost cost, a bad seed, so I could not understand what she wanted from me. I asked her don't you believe that my bad spirit would rub off on you, and she laugh and said I want you to come to church with me, I told her you must be crazy they do not want me at that church I am not allowed on the church grounds, and plus I would never go back there any way, She said I don't go there any more,

I go to a new church, I said no, because when I really needed Her she had turned her back on me, because of what man told her to do, and if I mess up again she would do it again, and I did not want to go through the rejection any more, but we talked,

she apologized for how she treated me and ask for forgiveness and told me she loved me and God had sent her to invite me to this church, Oh boy what do God want from me again? I said to myself, so after a few begs I said what do I have to lose, so I said yes, I still was feeling the pain of angry tears of losing everything in my life from a failed marriage, and not having a relationship with my mother, losing two brothers and not forgiving my father before he had past and I just had lost an uncle I loved dearly, and the lost of the only mother I had my adopted mother, and a nephew, my pain was so deep inside I was too scared to let anyone in, I was scared to be put out another church, I felt that I was marked with some type of seal, letting people know that I was a lose cost from birth.

I knew if I did not get myself together I was going to head down a road of destruction and instead of disappointing God again I rather die, and go to hell, so I started plotting my death again, I knew that I was weak and was scared to ask man to pray for me, I did not have enough strength to pray for myself, every time I tried I felt worst, so I deciding writing letters to my kids letting them know everything concerning my life and letting them know how much I loved them, I knew that she was coming to get me for church and I wanted to be gone before she arrived so I got some pills together,

And got myself together, so as a nurse I knew what to take to make my heart stop, it was time to let it all go, I read my bible before I decided to end all this pain, I wrote the letters to my kids, and then I had a long talk with God, I really did not know if God was listening or not, but I cried out anyway for the last time, right before I took over 95 pills, I started to write my last letter it was address to God.

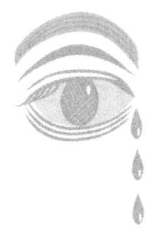

My Last Letter'

Lord please forgive me' for all I was not to you, forgive me for all my sins,

I know I would never be with you, or feel your hug or kiss, God I really did not want much, I did not want fame or riches, I did not want silver or gold, I did not want a house or a mansion, lord all I wanted was your love and forgiveness, lord all I wanted is you to be proud of calling me your child, lord all I wanted was your love, if I had your love God nothing in this world would of ever mattered, I am sorry lord that all I have been was a problem child, lord I understand why you never blessed me or kept me,

I am so sorry for the mess, I tried to clean it up lord, but it was too messy for me to handle alone, I am so sorry for reopening your wound, I know that you died for me so that I could have life, and all I ever done was brought you shame! But God I did believe you at your word and feared you that is why I rather died and go to hell then to bring rottenness to your bones,

lord my favorite scripture in your word is Proverbs 12 and verse 4, I wanted to be that virtuous woman, because if I was I would have been a crown to you, thank you for giving me another chance and I love you,

I really do, lord if I never see you please believe from the depths of my soul and the purity of my heart I am sorry for all my wrong doing, and please give your son Jesus a kiss from me if that is not too much to ask for, in Jesus name, after I prayed that prayer to the lord I took all my pills, I had taken 25 blood pressure pills, 30 pain pills, and 30 sleeping pills, I cut off all my lights and unplugged my phone and got into bed and my last words were.

God I rather die and go to hell then to live and sin against you again forgive me' for I know not what I have done in Jesus name! And I went to sleep.

Then I heard a voice say arise! Real firm it had shook my whole body! Then the voice came again saying arise my child,

your faith have made you whole, pick up your cross and follow me and never look back, for my love for you is greater than you can ever bare, all your sins have been forgiven and thrown in the sea of forgetfulness, for I have great works for you, and I know all about you and the angry tears, that you have shed before time, even before you were conceived in your mother belly, I gave you life to have it to the fullness, your weeping has endue for a night now your joy will be this morning, praise me in all that you do, tell everyone that Christ has risen in you, tell everyone of my goodness, for my child your life is only in my hands for the things you have endue was not to harm you but to make you strong and build you up for the purpose I have planned for you.

And Fret not of evildoers, but in all your ways acknowledge me' and I will direct your path.

Lean not unto your own understanding but allow me to lead you and guide you the rest of the journey, I loved you that's why I have chastening you for a long time!

Live again with the peace I am giving you, and live again in my name, I thought I was dreaming, until a bright light shine directly at me like I never seen before, I got up and started pitching myself to make sure I was not dead or dreaming, I started making phone calls to my love ones to see if this was real, I knew I had not gone to the hospital to have my stomach pumped, or I did not vomit the medicine, I looked around my floors they all were clean, nothing came up, I looked at all three bottles they were empty, I knew that I had taken the pills and being a nurse myself I knew that there was no way I could survive this without going to the hospital or something! So I got my blood pressure cuff out, and took my pressure it was one forty over eighty my temperature was normal and my skin was bright and shiny, I was walking and talking in my right mind, I started to shout out loud, giving God the glory saying lord you really love me, you really love me,

I danced all through the house, I wanted to tell everyone one what God had done for me, I knew if I told a doctor they would think that I was lying, or crazy, so I just got ready still looking for any signs of medical problem, a loud knock came at the door, it was my foster sister coming for me to go to the new church, she said you look different,

I smiled and got my coat and could not wait to get in a church to shout and testify about Gods miracle, and what the lord has done in me over and over again, as we drove to the church she said to me the lord told me that you are his anointed and he was going to use you in a mighty way, I laugh and said I receive that and believe that like I never done before. As we enter into the new church I felt like I have been here before' every one was so nice and I felt good entering into the church everyone gave me a hug like they knew what God had done for me in my life. Testimonies had started and I could not wait until I could scream out his blessing over the church, I started to say something but the spirit of God was all over me, and I just could not contain myself,

I praised the lord all over the church, I think I shouted out over a hundred times thank you lord, and giving him all the glory, and even danced my clothes off.

This was serious and personal to me' I praised the lord all that week. I loved reading Psalms, I loved how David was so grateful of God's Blessing over his life and for giving him another chance' I felt just like that, I knew that God was not silent toward me anymore, and the lord never walked away from me, I walked away from him, The lord loved me enough to save me from myself, I had been walking in darkness to long now my eyes were opened and I could see much brighter, in Matthew the lord lets us know that the gate is straight and narrow and if we go our way we would head for destruction, and that was what I was doing because I allowed my past to choose who and what I was and going to be, now I have a song in my heart, a dance in my feet and a shout in my mouth, because God told me in Hebrews chapter 12 verse 6 for whom I love I chasten, I knew then I was truly loved by God.

I found out that I had Agape love, unconditional, unselfish love, no matter what I have done in my life, he never turned his back on me, God is a forgiving God and Jesus had already died for the sins I did or going to do, he told me that in Romans chapter 3 verse chapter 23 that all have sinned and come short of the glory of God, and I thought that I was the only bad seed in the bunch, this is how I was miss leaded by man, I was rejected and abandoned and judge every time I made a mistake, rather it was big or small, but the lord was talking to me every day, I could hear his voice clearly, and he was letting me know in Psalms chapter 118 verse eight it is better not to put all your trust and confidence in man but put in the lord, The lord had let me know that he was the only one that knows the plans he has for me, and he wants to prosper me, and not harm me, but to give me hope and a future in him.

As I read my word daily he spoke this to me in Jeremiah chapter 29 verses 11. It was so hard in my past to hear from God when I first gave my life to him because I was moving faster than my spirit was taking me,

The lord let me know that I got to be still and see the salvation of the lord work in my life and it was a process not when I want it, but when I needed it, it was going to be on time,

I need to grow and develop a relationship with him first' before I could expect to have or receive it from anyone else, I had to be in my proper place at the proper time, to see the works of God manifest in my life, I need a real solid foundation relationship with the lord so when the trials and tribulations come I would be in a firm position, so when I do fall I would be able to get right back up.

I joined the church and was growing daily with my the studies they had, and the studies I were doing at home with God, I was falling in love with the lord and learning how to love and forgive, starting with myself, I had to forgive myself first, then I found myself forgiving my mother, father, foster parents, uncles, and even the men that hurt me in my life that took advantage of me. The lord was teaching me how to love myself, and to be a person he had made me to be in his own image,

I had to start back with that little girl, the lord showed me in his word. In Genesis chapter 1 verse 26, he states let's make man in his own image, in his likeness for God to make me in his own image. I know that I was very special. God told me that I had to be tested and go through some things because of the call I had over my life.

And then I read the story concerning Job in the bible the word then spoke to me letting me know that If Satan could destroy me, the purpose that was already planned for my life would not be, only if I gave up and not believe, if Job went through everything I read in the word of God how he believed and had faith to know that no matter what comes or go he would trust in the lord till the day he die, and then how his trust in God bless him more than he could ever imagine, then why can't I hang in there a little while longer knowing that the enemy works are to seek as a thief to come to steal, and kill, and to destroy,

This is what he had set out for me as a child to steal my identity by letting my mind believe that I was dome from the start' allowing me to believe I was ugly, and was never going to nothing in life or anyone else, And everyone would look at me as a trouble problem child, I was believing that I would never be a child of God, I tried to kill myself by trying to take my own life, I felt neglected, abandoned, I was emotionally, mentally and physically abused, I was trick to believe I was full of lust, loneliness, envy, jealousy, full of lies, but thank the lord he had his hand on my life all along. As I spent more time with God I received my learning and the word taught me daily by killing the my flesh daily, I know that the devil would try to discredit the lord's word and his job was to destroy that belief, in John chapter 5 verse 36 tells us that if we believe in his son we will have everlasting life, and Acts chapter 16 verse 31 also let us know to believe in the lord Jesus Christ we shall be save and our household,

This last attempt I have been running for the lord it is now 2006 and everything is good I still been having trials and tribulations but reading my word daily fasting and praying and talking to God developing the relation I need with him falling in love with my lord and savior it has been three years and living alone without a man in my life was great,

I meet a good man of God my bible study partner we loved doing ministry for the lord and a man that was really after God's own heart, this walk with God was sweeter than the day before, one day I was going to the store and was at the counter and a man behind me ask for change and I turned around to give him a dollar and it was the man that had took my brother life, the brother that I loved dearly, my heart stopped beating, but all I could do is hand him the dollar and walked to my car with feeling compassion for him, I sat in my car for a minute and thanked God because at a time in my life I had planned to kill this man for taking someone I love so dearly away, the enemy tried me at this moment wanting me to run him over with my car,

But I called on the name of Jesus to give me strength as he walked out the store I asked him if he needed a ride and he got in my car not knowing or remembering that I was the sister of the man he killed, I asked him was he saved and he said no, I told him that God loves him and forgave him and I forgive him too, he looked at me and remembered and said you are tee-bone sister and I said yes with a tear in his eye he said I am so sorry, pray for me.

And I gave him a hug and gave him a church to go to and told him don't let it be too late. I knew then that God was making a change in my life, after hating this man for so many years,

I could not find that hate I had' all I felt was compassion for him and wanted to help this man, Glory be to God.

I thank God all the way home, because if God did not step in right on time, I would have been in prison or somewhere. Thank you Lord for saving me, I prayed all that week for that young man that God bless him, I knew then I was changed.

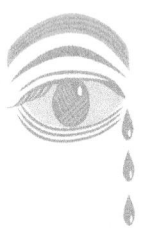

Chapter 9

Renewed but same Tears!

My mind was being renewed and God was still working on me. As a child I did not realize that God had his hand on my life, all I ever seen was the darkness that was given to me, no light that shine in my life. I am an older woman now with grown children and grandchildren and just experiencing true love a love that no other could give or take, a love that God gave' his only begotten son so I can have this life. I am having now, what a love that someone could show to lay down his life for his people, not my mother, nor my father, not my brother or sister, friends nor any of my family ever shown or gave this type of love.

To know that God has set us up in heavenly places with Jesus Christ some day, you see all the time he loved me, and still do, but when you are in darkness and have not seen any light you can't see, feel or taste any love, only temporary loves that comes and goes all the time.

But the love from God is real he will never turn his back on you, he loved me through it all, when I was not patience, when I did not want to repent, when I was being bad, when I shut the doors on him,

When I served Satan time after time after time, even when I didn't even love myself, he loved me, even when I cursed my life he had given me, he loved me, even when I thought that I have accomplished things on my own, he loved me, even when I told him that I hated him, he loved me, when I spited on him, laughed at him, and even nailed him to the cross by rejecting who he was, denying his love for me, the lord never gave up on me.

I can tell you this because he forgave me, he protected me, he trust me with his word, because he believed in me, because he preserved my soul, because he never failed me yet, because he threw all my sins in the sea of forgetfulness.

I was a broken vessel and the lord looked down from heaven and breath life of everlasting in me, and said I shall live and not die, the devil had to get permission to do what he had done to me, but the lord demanded him like he did Job don't touch her soul' that belongs to me, just to know that made me realize that God never left my side, now tell me who do you know that will stand by you all the way? Grace and mercy has followed me all the days of my life, and still is today. If we don't have hope then what do we have? I always heard growing up keep hope alive? That's true but without keeping Jesus alive in you then you got no hope to keep! All I had to do is repent ask God to forgive me and live the way he design for me to live, study my word, develop a relationship with the lord, receive Christ in my life, believe his word, then I would be born again, then I would receive the instruction on how to overcome the affliction that would attack my flesh, because the spirit would fight my battle for me, all I had to do is surrender the dark pain, the angry tears, I had reserved from the devil and give it all to Jesus,

I could of saved myself a lot of unnecessary chaos.

I believed what others spoke on my life, which made me so confuse' one moment I was an bad seed, and in another breathe I was a bless seed, I would say to myself can God make up his mind of who, what I am, but through it all I learn that if you don't believe who you are in Christ then you would believe anything the devil speaks about you.

If we truly believe in God' then why is so hard to believe him at his word? Our own knowledge is not the knowledge of God, but we can receive it, in Matthew Chapter 7 verse 8 says everyone that asked received, so ask for knowledge, ask for wisdom, ask for understanding, God will open the door for you, this is the main reason why Gods people is being destroyed every day because of being fools to the lack of knowledge.

If we would just pick up our bibles everyday and read more than a Sunday or Bible study night' than we would find more treasures to our solutions on dealing with daily traumas,

Yes God does gives to the pastors, leaders, prophets, teachers, evangelists, but he also gives to you, so that your spirits would come into agreements on where God is taking and bringing you from, 2Timothy chapter 2 verse 15 tells us to study to show thyself approved only unto God, so that we would not be blind or deceived by the enemy traps by false Prophets that will come in the name of Jesus Christ. I was so guilty of that, I would go to church listen to what the pastor preached and on and TV ministries and just read daily bread and hearing the word through other people, I was just too lazy to pick up my bible and read for myself, the lord had to show me that you just don't go out and eat from everyone breakfast, lunch, dinner or snack table, we need to prepare our own food at times so that we can put in the right ingredients, so we will be able to digest it the right way and the taster the spiritual man would be able to know that we can cook too. I had to remember that I was being prepared to be God's bride as well, and how would I want to come prepared? Done or under cooked?

As I allow my spiritual man to be fed the right things I seen a change and growth on how I dealt with my trials and tribulations, Matthew chapter 20 verse 14 tells us that many are called but only a few are chosen to lead God's people, so it is very important to read and study the word daily so when the test's come you would not faint or give in, when I starting letting go and let God I started seeing my angry tears being wiped away, it was so hard for me to believe that the word of God was real because I have seen so many leaders and family members mock the word so much, until God manifest himself to me, the lord has opened up my eyes everyday and the light gets brighter and brighter every day.

I have put my trust in man to long, believing when they tell me I am not save' I believe it, when I made mistakes over and over again I was not a child of God, I believe it, when I spoke my mind when my spirit did not agree what they would say concerning my life, I was rebellious, I believed it, in their eyes I was not good enough or I was another failure because I did not walk, talk, jump or say how high, I did not look a certain way, I was not important enough, I believed it.

But the Lord let me know a different song to the dance in his word Ephesians chapter 2 verse 5 says His Grace saves me, and in Romans chapter 3verse 23 he also tells me that we all have sinned and Come short of the glory of God, I am not what man says I am but I am what God says I am, and that is I am more than a conqueror because of his love, what a great identity to receive from God himself, thank you Jesus.

All thing are new and the old is passed away, I can look at life the way God had me to look at it through his eyes, my tears still come but they are not the angry ones, I can rejoice' and praise him through my walk, the lord has turned my sorrow into joy, I had no faith, I had no joy, I had no hope and no peace, but look at me know I got the victory, sometimes we got to be broken so that we could realize that we cannot be made whole again until receive and believe that we need Jesus, when I look back over my life as a little girl I can truly say I am bless, and when I look back over my life as a young woman I can say I am truly bless, when I look back over my life as a woman today I can truly say that I am bless,

I have a mighty awesome bless testimony to share to this world. If you don't believe that Satan is a reality then keep reading this book over and over and over until you get it, but know that God is realist.

Yes the lord is still working on and in me, he is washing me daily, you see I was just living my life in a way I thought was pleasing to me to be happy, but all I was doing was destroying my destiny with filthy things inside of me and believe me it was many, I had an abuse spirit, adultery spirit, anger spirit, anxiety spirit, low self esteem spirit, attitude spirit, backsliding spirit, bad habit spirit, bitterness spirit, deceit spirit, depression spirit, discouragement spirit, doubt spirit, enemies spirit, envy spirit, fame spirit, fear spirit, flattery spirit, gambling spirit, gossip spirit, grief spirit, guilt spirit, incest spirit, laziness spirit, loneliness spirit, lust spirit, occult spirit, pride spirit, revenge spirit, self pity spirit, shame spirit, lying spirit, and the list goes on, sometimes we believe that we go to church and one thing we don't do like we should is repent with a repenting heart any more,

We feel that we are okay because no one knows the deep dark secrets, but the devil is a lie because God knows all and see all nothing is hidden from him,

Every time we turn our backs on God and go another way we picks up more demotic spirits and it is more harder than when we first gave our life to Christ.

Some of us now feel that we are okay because no one around us knows are deep dark secrets, don't you know we sit down on someone's else deliverance because of that fear we have deep down inside to not let ourselves be totally free from shame, and blame, there will be and are not any perfect person, but we can build into Gods family that can be made into perfection if we let go and let God, God can heal all broken vessels, there is nothing to hard for God, It does not take over night for your process to happen, but if you put your time in believe me payday is on the way, stop going to these get your miracles today and that's it, and go to the real place God's house, and wait on your blessing!

Romans chapter 14 verse 12 the lord tells that everyone shall give an account of him or herself to him no matter what someone else has done or said to you, and read 2 Corinthians chapter 5 verse 10, everyone may receive the things done in his or her body according to what our actions are whether it is good or bad, and every time I backslid' I gave the enemy more closet space to hang his garments for me to wear, know that the flesh got to die daily' your soul is what God demands the devil not to touch, so go through it' it is worth it at the end, it is very hard to suffer but know that the longsuffering is molding you into the image of God and in his likeness.

Just know that the fruit is being replanted from bad soil to good soil and this time when it grows it is going to bloom into the flower we were meant to be in the beginning, plan time with God' I decided that I rather be born twice than to die once.

It is so funny I remember when I first came to Jesus I heard this song come to Jesus, come to Jesus, come to Jesus right now, he will save me, from all I went through and going through they let me believe that I would not suffer any more.

I would not shed a tear any more, he has forgiven me, and all my problems were gone, My life would be so much better, no more worries; all my troubles would be over, I would have peace joy and happiness, I would be bless with lots of things, and all I heard was just that, but they forgot to let me know that Jesus had paid for all that with his blood by being beaten, lied on, talked about, spit on, dragged, rejected, tempted, and nailed to his cross that he had to carry, the enemy hated Jesus' so what make us think that we did not have a cross to carry! Everything you go through for righteous sake, because It is only a test, the battle is already won' You can will make it, just trust, believe and have faith as long as you are living for the lord you can bear these things,

I will be able to endure it all with the strength of God, know that you are save by his grace, And all the lord ask in return, ourselves, this flesh do not mean us no good, pick up your cross no matter how hard it is, and allow Jesus to help you carry it to the end, we have a test to go through, a test that helps us to our destiny, Don't let the devil defeat you, know that God is the master of it all.

God knows what he needs to do to get us where we need to go, and where we need to be, 1Peter chapter 1verse 7 tells us that our trails of our faith being more precious than anything that perish going through the fire might be praise and honor and glory when Jesus comes for you, and Revelation Chapter 2 verse 10 tell us not to fear none of these things that we suffer, it is the devil job to cast some of us into prison, that we be tried and have tribulations,

But for us to be faithful because God has a great crown of life for us, the enemy wants us to believe that we will not make it, this is it for us, but we know that Satan is the father and creator of lies and the truth is not in him,

Hold on to the little faith that you got and allow God to uncover your victory, I am still holding on waiting and enjoying my walk with the lord, yes I am still going through, yes I have fallen short, yes my mind wonders if I am going to make it, but when I truly think about the goodness of Jesus and all that he has pulled me from, and see the true call on my life my soul just screams toward the finish line, by me studying the word of God and developing a relationship with the lord helped saved my life,

Reading Psalms chapter 5 verse 3 trained me how to ask God for his help. Reading Lamentations Chapter 3 verse 23 helps me to know Gods faithfulness and how his mercy I need every day. Because when my trails comes it would only be the test of my faith in him, oh believe me it will still come until that day of the lord return, but I know that the battle is already won.

There is a road that we need to follow called the highway to heaven, and it is straight and narrow, there are no left or right turns, but if you get side tracked you can make a u – turn and get back on the right road, so when the persecution occur know that it is only planned to build the faith of the image we see a head, Jesus!

Every day I got to give him the praise no matter what I am going through knowing that I was nothing but a dirty filthy rag, and God is using me as a precious gift wrapped with a lot of blessings that is precious in his sight.

All my life I was program to believe that I was a walking dead, too late to help human being, the devil had me wrapped up tangle up in sin, but the escape was the key of choice! God had hand delivered it to me in the right box called you shall live and not die,

I remember when I came out of the coma people would ask me about life after death, and I really did not know how to answer that, until now, I am life after death' a new woman in Christ,

I was dead to sin, now I am alive in Christ, having love, joy, peace, longsuffering, gentleness, goodness, faith, meekness, and temperance.

You know every time I think about where the lord has brought me from, the things I go through now should be easy' but sometime we forget the blessings of his grace & mercy, when other trails comes, I know when I was being afflicted with being in a wheelchair, being bed bond,

using 24 hours oxygen to breathe, when my body was so bend up into knots, when my body was racking with pain, I was on every medication that was new on the market that they could give me, when I had several nervous breakdowns being depressed, people betting on my life rather I was going to live or die.

When people wonder why I haven't lost my mind yet, It was all God' 2 Peter chapter 2 verse 24 tells us that Jesus himself bared our sins on the cross so that we being dead to sins should live unto righteousness, and by his stripes we are healed,

I was already healed before my time, whatever afflictions my flesh endued is dead, and cannot do me any harm I am healed through Christ that dwells in me' And when I thought that hope was all gone, when I was not accepted and my church family turned their backs on me, I thought I would not be accepted into another church, by having my name slandered and being an social outcast, the lord gave me comfort in the mist of it all, and minister to my soul in Romans chapter 10 verse 11 he spoke for whosoever believe in me shall not be ashamed, and in Psalm chapter 55 verse 22 cast all your burdens upon me said the lord and I shall sustain you, the lord would never let us suffer for his righteous to be removed, when we are being cursed we will be bless, when we are being persecuted we can endure it, when we are being slander for his name sake we answer kindly.

For the battle is not ours it is the lords.

Being a divorce woman bothered me a lot until the lord let me know that I needed to be married to him first, and be taught how to become a wife, I needed more cleansing from my past, more training, more molding,

I need to know how to love myself first, be faithful, be loyal, be honest, be patient, be wise, be obedient, and longsuffering, I had to be approved and sealed by God first'

believe me I had none of these things not even a crumb, some of us get married because of past failure like me, loneliness, lust, finance for all the wrong reason, but how can you love and want to spend our life with someone when we hate ourselves? And we lack all our time with God, we can't even be in a relation with God so how can we do it with a man or female?

We need to call on the clean up power' and that is God' So we will not be left behind' due to lack of knowledge when the lord appears, I received peace after my divorce, the lord is doing a great work in me, yes I am still in training with the spirit of God to be what I need to be for my maker, my creator, do be all that I need to be in him and for him, so if you what a husband or seeking to be a wife this is what God told me in Isaiah chapter 54 verse 5 thy maker is the husband the lord of host is his name, and thy redeemer, the holy one, the God of the whole earth shall he be called, So every time I get a itch that forms with someone saying little nothings in my ear I remember the word in 1Corinthians chapter 6 verse 18 thru 20 tells me to flee from fornication, every one that commits fornication sinned against his own body, and that our bodies are the temple in which the holy spirit dwells in and the holy spirit does not dwells in an unclean temple, and that we belong to God.

We are brought with a price so therefore glorify God in your body and in your spirit, just like his word say in 1Thessalonians chapter 4 verse 3 this is the will of God, that we should abstain from fornication, believe me it might be hard but it is worth it when you know what he tells us in James chapter 1 verse 12, bless is the man the endured temptation for when he is tried, he shall receive the crown of life which the lord hath promised to them that love and keeps his commandments. And believe me it is still a battle, but I refuse to turn back now or give up, the lord has brought me too far, for me to not hold on just a little longer.

This is why it is so important for us that go through or have been through so much turmoil's in our past or present to tell yourself, train yourself, to feast on the word morning, noon and night,

Even for a midnight snack, so that when the enemy arise with some type of mess you will be able to resist and make a stand for what is right, go through' but don't entertain. I had to do the same thing and still calling on the lord name,

I truly thank God every time I wake up, and decided to follow Jesus through it all. We have a cover if we want it, and that is the blood of Jesus, and believe me there is a warning precautious sign telling us to stop, yield, don't go, or enter at your own risk! We cannot put down any part of the whole Armor of God, for any reason!

How can you go to battle with good looks, or with holding things that has your hands full sometimes your hands need to be free, that is why we need the word in our hearts so that when the enemy comes at you and see you empty handed you are equipped in heart, mind and soul, and know that you need it every day when you walk with God!

When you start your journey toward your destiny don't start tired, sleepy and unprepared, like the five foolish virgins, have your lamp full, let your light shine all the way, until you get to your destination.

Because the enemy hates to lose and he will keep coming back, he wants to destroy your destiny your purpose your plan that God has for you, so always be on guard, but fret not there is nothing he can do to you that God has not okay, he needs permission, so look' If he got permission to attack, then know that God has elevated you to overcome.

Don't think that I have it all together because I don't, but I got someone in my corner that does! Jesus Christ! What more do I need? It is now 2005 and I had a flood come toward me, my faith was being tried again my real biological mother was ill' I was running up and down the high way from Ohio to New York seeing about her, I really did not know what was wrong,

I had started a ministry for the youth in my community back in 2004 sharing some of my testimony, spending time, teaching them about God and having children Church, it was so fulfilling with no help from others me and my daughter just doing what the lord put in us to do,

Sharing the love of Jesus to these children was awesome. I used all my disability check monthly for uniforms supplies, gas, food, and field trips to these youth I did not care what it cost me I did what my heart lead me to do, with the help of my daughter we maintain through God help, some were children from bad and good back ground, we help elderly, we went to hospitals, nursing home and group homes to share the love of Jesus, I would load up 20 kids in a little car I had and just prayed that the Lord provide us there and back, it was sad that my community never step in to give a hand, but I was not discouraged because they never helped when I was a child in need,

So I pushed myself with God on my side and did what I had to do, with going back and forth to New York it was hard people did not care to step in to help a small group of children that needed love and compassion, I guess it was too much work, but I did what I had to do, my mother got sicker and I decided to bring her here instead and care for her at my home, the doctors did not believe she would,make it that far but I put all my trust in the lord and knew that God still had something for me and my mother to do,

And that was building a relationship, and to forgive before my next step in ministry that was coming around the corner, building families in forgiving their past and parents, God had called me to teach women from all types of family problems, I knew this was a set up from God to build my mother and I relationship, because how can I teach something I have not been through myself!

Because we never spent time together and forgave one another, I always loved my mother deep down inside, no matter what she did or said, or did not do for me. It was something I needed to move forward to the calling God had for me.

Believe me my family was not to thrill about me bringing my mother here, because of some past hidden pain they never faced, but God help me do the right thing, because I had some deep pain inside that was hunting me, and hindering me from moving forward, even though thing were going great in ministry I still had some angry tears that were still trying to be wiped.

I still blamed her for the death of my brother, my rape and being molested, for my failed relationship with men, my failure of being a good mother, my failure of never having a relationship with family members, for me not loving myself and me hating her, I still had some hidden scares, even through God has given me another chance and delivered me from some things,

I still had this deep dark angry tear that would not leave I needed a mother, touch, love and approval.

Why because in God's word he lets us know that he if the father to the fatherless and a mother to the motherless. So I went and got my mother and had to deal with a lot of medical problems, but I did what I had to do as her child and a child of God, I wanted all my actions to be pleasing to God so I prayed daily for the strength of God to help me do the right thing, without any bitterness in my heart, my baby sister was here at the time, but she was on drugs and she could not be of good help, my mother had sisters but because of past pain it stop them from stepping in like they needed to, so I prayed and did what my heart told me to do, and that is forgive first, love and be the child of God I am, I hated to see her in so much pain, always in and out of the hospital, I really had my hands full with the ministry, my relation with God, and my children and grandchildren, and taking care of my health too, and a sick mother, God just step in and gave the extra hand I needed.

I cried many of days because my mother heart was still harden toward me, I screamed inside a lot because whatever and how ever I did it she would complain, I got angry because she would lie and backbit against me, but I did not sin against her, she made feel like she still hated me, but God held my hand, he lifted me up and carried me through it all, she would cause division between me and my children and my baby sister, but God kissed me and sang a new song in my spirit, she spit all type of venom at me, but God washed me and gave me the strength and courage to hold on, In spite of what was fighting in her I knew that it was the enemy doings.

The lord had me minister to her daily and show her that her anger and pain that she had was hindering her from her real break- through, it was only her test to pull through or be destroy in it,

And God wants to deliver her so that he can bless her and heal her from all your infirmities, it was so hard for me to bath, feed and nursery a woman that seemed to hate me, my grandmother never agreed for me to care for my mother, but she still prayed for me and always encourage me to have a relationship with her. Some of my aunts wanted me to put her in a nursing home, but I remember my baby sister said to me sis it is better you than me to care for her, but God had order this day, this time.

And this season, for his reasons so I followed his instructions. As time went by I was still doing the ministry the lord had birth in me then he took the ministry to another level.

But when you are going through things and others are taking you through, sometimes the enemy would allow you to think that your past is back and having you doubt God at his word.

Sometimes he would make you believe that this is the worst test you are going through, but know that It is only a test of your faith, the higher you go, the higher the devil need to pull you down, because he is no longer welcome in heaven,

And when you are going through everyone that gave you advice to fail is gone, but know that God would never leave you nor forsake you. He will be there through the good and the bad,

one morning I was going through and wanted to totally give up with caring for my mother and the lord spoke to me through his word, Deuteronomy chapter 31 verse 6, he said be of good courage, fear not, nor be afraid of them, for the lord thy God do good in you, he will never fail you nor fake you, and in Romans chapter 15 verse 13, he said that he will fill me with Joy and Peace in my Deliverance, I would have hope through the power of the Holy Ghost that is in me,

And then he went on by saying in Philippians chapter 4 verse 7 that his peace would give me understanding and God will guard my heart and my mind as long as I keep my belief in him.

The lord was so busy helping me that day building my faith up in him, I knew that my mother would be okay and I would too, and to love her through it all, my grandmother always said just love the hell out of people, and if I had to love the hell out of my mother and love Jesus in her then that was my plan to hang in there, because in Isaiah chapter 26 verses 3 the lord will give me perfect peace just trust him, when I started looking over the hills, which comes my help and knew that my help was only going to come from the lord I was strong I truly felt the strength of the lord rising up in me.

Now it is time to slow down a little in ministry, I was kind of mad because I loved getting up and doing for others, but the condition of my mother was getting bad and was in greater need,

And God was doing a thing with us both he was moving me into another level in ministering to woman and I was getting woman that was not in good relationships with their Mothers and I was not there yet with my own, so how could the blind lead the blind?

So I removed myself to get what Jesus needed for me to have before I moved into my next assignment, at this time I had meet a young man that was interested in me, I meet him at a church singing and the lord spoke to me at this time letting me know that this man was my husband and I laugh at the lord saying lord I have no time for any man especially a husband, what are you talking about?

I am just fine, I love just being your wife and you my man and I have a friend, if I am lonely I got someone to pray with, talk with, go to dinner with, and to yell at, I laugh' because I had always talked to God like he was and is my best friend since I develop a relationship with him'

This was the end of 2005, I ignored the voice of God because I was so happy with my life in Jesus, I did not want anything to interfere with the love I had for God.

This male ministry was singing at this church at the time and I was walking out the door and the spirit of God spoke again saying go and give him a kiss on the check for me and let him know that I love him, and it will be okay, I said to myself lord are you okay? I will not touch that man, he would think I want him and I am okay, then the lord ask me if you love me and obey me like you say then you would trust what I am saying, I was kind of mad, but I obeyed the voice of God, I walked back into the church and walked over to the young man and gave him a hug and kissed him on the cheek and told him that God loves him and it will be okay, he looked at me with a surprise look, with a smile like he knew what I was saying was true, he said thank you, and I went on my way I kind of laughed to myself and said lord you are off the hook' At this time I went home and me and my mother was talking about some things in my past, my mother never wanted to hear about the past she would get upset and did not want to deal with what she did or cause, so I just prayed that God would let her know that she got to face some things before God could release her to her future.

She was in denial, she knew it was true, but she wanted to leave it behind without forgiving or ask for forgiveness.

So I started taking her to the church I was going to and she loved it she started seeing the spirit of God move in people life's, then she started getting involved and in 2006 she gave her life to Christ. Even though she gave her life it still was some things God needed to do in her, she still had something in her that hinder her from loving me totally.

Well me and this man I meet in church started to communicate more that I met, and everything was not that great in this man all he ever did was jump from woman to woman and he was a good man deep down inside, and we had a lot in common, many times I had to go to God and say lord I know you don't have this man for me' because he got too much work that need to be done in him for me to deal with, but we became best friends, I would talk to him a lot concerning my struggles and he would open up to me concerning his, it was hard to really date him, but we was good friends because of his life style with too many other women that would put a red flag up, but I would always encourage him to read his word and let God love him the way he need to be love, we really had a lot in common, his loneliness and wanted to be love and someone to love him,

I remember when I felt that way, our back ground was kind of the same but he was raised with his parent and he was not abused, but he did feel not supported to become success in his life, but I would encourage him with my testimony to let him know it was never too late for God to change and arrange him in what God is calling him to be. A Godly man first. This man had a good heart deep down inside, it was just all over the place.

But for some reason God connected us together, I just did not see my self-being his wife, at least at that time. But we enjoyed each other company, well now It is 2007 and my mother is still holding on, still fighting this sickness she has in and out of hospitals and nursing home, I prayed every day that God would bless her, we started spending more time like a mother and daughter should, I loved my mother, we had some ups and down but our relationship became stronger, even with all her the hurt she afflicted me with, I found myself loving her through it all.

I had a great help in dealing with what I was going through, a mother of the church that had twelve boys told me one day "no matter what we go through or what people have done to us we got to have a different approach", we got to still give love as children of God, we only would have "one mother" that God has given no matter how many play a role as a mother

God gave us our parents to respect and if we obey the word of God we will see the true blessing in that. It made me think that no matter what happen I got through because of the seed God implant within me, and maybe something happened in my mother past that cost her traumas that intervene in caring for me and my brother, and some generational curses are to be broken and not mended back together, my mother started being a friend to me even with the hidden backstabbing at this time, I really did not care I just wanted to love her and forgive her and be the daughter she needed me to be. I really would not understand her pain, only God! I don't know what she has been through.

But I was here for her in case she wanted to open up, I just wanted her to know that she was forgiven and I loved her no matter what.

So this brother and I relationship got serious, he was singing for God and I was called to preach and teach his word, we became closer as time went by, he helped me a lot in caring for my mother, but there was always some type of issue he had, woman! Because I was saving myself for God right time in for my life, he did not totally understand that because of the women he dated allowed him to stay and live and sleep with them, and these women were in church like I was, but as time went by I explain to him some of my past so he could understand, I gave him scriptures to look up so he would understand about the temple of God, I hated to see him in this type of web that the devil was holding him in, so I prayed for his deliverance, I asked God why the man I was friends with for four years never tried or ask to touch me and we spent lots and more time together than the man you say would be my husband?

One preaches the word and the other sang the word?

But as time went by I understood that the enemy had deceived him so many times and all he ever wanted was to be love and God was the one that was going to give it to him and I needed to be patient and see the salvation of God move.

Sometime we give up on people before God tells us to, and a lot of us miss out on our true blessings.

The crazy thing about being with him, was that it would hurt him to even hear that I went through the things I went through, and his heart was so much in making me happy, pleasing me, talking to me like the lord would have some do, but I rejected it a lot because of his short comings of wanting me to love him not only mentally but physically, and I was not going to take it to that level,

But we remained good friends through it all,

I was always was in and out of town working for the lord, to tell you the truth I never had a man that shared tears with me and cared that much about what happen to me even my friend from church did not do that, so I knew he had some form of heart God in him,

He just did not know how to really let go and let God work it out for him, he did not know about the Holy Spirit that comes in and live in you, the power he needed to change some things in him. No one ever took the time to explain or teach him what the word of God says about this type of activity. So the devil knew his weakness and tried to destroy him with it, but we know God is always on time.

Well it is 2007 still hanging in there with mom and this new love I got in my life but still depending on God for what I need and want, ministry was strong it had its ups and down, but we know that everyone that call On the name can also be full of game,

The lord was using me in ways I never could of imagine, my life testimony helped a lot of people and the relationships, what I had with my mom, helped delivered other daughters and mothers.

At this time I was going through a lot because my mother health had truly turned to the worst, her health had put her in intensive care and I was so busy running back and forth to the hospital, not knowing but holding on to faith that God would pull her through, I needed a little more time with my mother, It still was things I needed to talk to her about, and at this time I did get a little weak in my walk with God, my man friend was going through some things so we feed off each other strength, I allowed him to move in to help him out for awhile at this time, I felt that I was doing the right thing, I hated to see anyone in need, like I used to be, and if I had it I would share to the world no matter who it was.

But my spirit was warning me and I just did not believe I would fall into temptation.

I felted strong enough in the lord to sustain myself from any temptation, so I thought'

But who were I fooling we were sharing too much time together, then the kissing came from time to time, then the hugging and the love taps, lord help me please! I never felt the feelings I felt with him, I thought we would be safe as long as I kept on praying, finally I could not contain myself, he started telling me that he wanted to spend the rest of his life with me and he needed a woman like me, and I remember that God said that this man was going to be my husband, and I just let all the guards I had down, I never had a man that stayed home at night cooked, cleaned ran my bath water, loved kids, listened to me,

I just thought well lord forgive me even though the love making was good, but what happen to God commandments, I felt like I just died, I never wanted to let God down again, I really wanted to make it until the time was right.

Chapter 10

Strength to Care

I had started a ministry for the youth in my community back in 2004 sharing some of my testimony, spending time, teaching them about God and having children Church, it was so fulfilling with no help from others me and my daughter just doing what the lord put in us to do,

Sharing the love of Jesus to these children was awesome. I used all my disability check monthly for uniforms supplies, gas, food, and field trips to these youth I did not care what it cost me I did what my heart lead me to do, with the help of my daughter we maintain through God help, some were children from bad and good back ground, we help elderly, we went to hospitals, nursing home and group homes to share the love of Jesus, I would load up 20 kids in a little car I had and just prayed that the Lord provide us there and back, it was sad that my community never step in to give a hand, but I was not discouraged because they never helped when I was a child in need,

So I pushed myself with God on my side and did what I had to do, with going back and forth to New York it was hard people did not care to step in to help a small group of children that needed love and compassion, I guess it was too much work, but I did what I had to do, my mother got sicker and I decided to bring her here instead and care for her at my home, the doctors did not believe she would,make it that far but I put all my trust in the lord and knew that God still had something for me and my mother to do,

And that was building a relationship, and to forgive before my next step in ministry that was coming around the corner, building families in forgiving their past and parents, God had called me to teach women from all types of family problems, I knew this was a set up from God to build my mother and I relationship, because how can I teach something I have not been through myself!

Because we never spent time together and forgave one another, I always loved my mother deep down inside, no matter what she did or said, or did not do for me. It was something I needed to move forward to the calling God had for me.

Believe me my family was not to thrill about me bringing my mother here, because of some past hidden pain they never faced, but God help me do the right thing, because I had some deep pain inside that was hunting me, and hindering me from moving forward, even though thing were going great in ministry I still had some angry tears that were still trying to be wiped.

I still blamed her for the death of my brother, my rape and being molested, for my failed relationship with men, my failure of being a good mother, my failure of never having a relationship with family members, for me not loving myself and me hating her, I still had some hidden scares, even through God has given me another chance and delivered me from some things,

I still had this deep dark angry tear that would not leave I needed a mother, touch, love and approval.

Why because in God's word he lets us know that he if the father to the fatherless and a mother to the motherless. So I went and got my mother and had to deal with a lot of medical problems, but I did what I had to do as her child and a child of God, I wanted all my actions to be pleasing to God so I prayed daily for the strength of God to help me do the right thing, without any bitterness in my heart, my baby sister was here at the time, but she was on drugs and she could not be of good help, my mother had sisters but because of past pain it stop them from stepping in like they needed to, so I prayed and did what my heart told me to do, and that is forgive first, love and be the child of God I am, I hated to see her in so much pain, always in and out of the hospital, I really had my hands full with the ministry, my relation with God, and my children and grandchildren, and taking care of my health too, and a sick mother, God just step in and gave the extra hand I needed.

I cried many of days because my mother heart was still harden toward me, I screamed inside a lot because whatever and how ever I did it she would complain, I got angry because she would lie and backbit against me, but I did not sin against her, she made feel like she still hated me, but God held my hand, he lifted me up and carried me through it all, she would cause division between me and my children and my baby sister, but God kissed me and sang a new song in my spirit, she spit all type of venom at me, but God washed me and gave me the strength and courage to hold on, In spite of what was fighting in her I knew that it was the enemy doings.

The lord had me minister to her daily and show her that her anger and pain that she had was hindering her from her real break- through, it was only her test to pull through or be destroy in it,

And God wants to deliver her so that he can bless her and heal her from all your infirmities, it was so hard for me to bath, feed and nursery a woman that seemed to hate me, my grandmother never agreed for me to care for my mother, but she still prayed for me and always encourage me to have a relationship with her. Some of my aunts wanted me to put her in a nursing home, but I remember my baby sister said to me sis it is better you than me to care for her, but God had order this day, this time.

And this season, for his reasons so I followed his instructions. As time went by I was still doing the ministry the lord had birth in me then he took the ministry to another level.

But when you are going through things and others are taking you through, sometimes the enemy would allow you to think that your past is back and having you doubt God at his word.

Sometimes he would make you believe that this is the worst test you are going through, but know that It is only a test of your faith, the higher you go, the higher the devil need to pull you down, because he is no longer welcome in heaven,

And when you are going through everyone that gave you advice to fail is gone, but know that God would never leave you nor forsake you. He will be there through the good and the bad, one morning I was going through and wanted to totally give up with caring for my mother and the lord spoke to me through his word, Deuteronomy chapter 31 verse 6, he said be of good courage, fear not, nor be afraid of them, for the lord thy God do good in you, he will never fail you nor fake you, and in Romans chapter 15 verse 13, he said that he will fill me with Joy and Peace in my Deliverance, I would have hope through the power of the Holy Ghost that is in me,

And then he went on by saying in Philippians chapter 4 verse 7 that his peace would give me understanding and God will guard my heart and my mind as long as I keep my belief in him.

The lord was so busy helping me that day building my faith up in him, I knew that my mother would be okay and I would too, and to love her through it all, my grandmother always said just love the hell out of people, and if I had to love the hell out of my mother and love Jesus in her then that was my plan to hang in there, because in Isaiah chapter 26 verses 3 the lord will give me perfect peace just trust him, when I started looking over the hills, which comes my help and knew that my help was only going to come from the lord I was strong I truly felt the strength of the lord rising up in me.

Now it is time to slow down a little in ministry, I was kind of mad because I loved getting up and doing for others, but the condition of my mother was getting bad and was in greater need,

And God was doing a thing with us both he was moving me into another level in ministering to woman and I was getting woman that was not in good relationships with their Mothers and I was not there yet with my own, so how could the blind lead the blind?

So I removed myself to get what Jesus needed for me to have before I moved into my next assignment, at this time I had meet a young man that was interested in me, I meet him at a church singing and the lord spoke to me at this time letting me know that this man was my husband and I laugh at the lord saying lord I have no time for any man especially a husband, what are you talking about?

I am just fine, I love just being your wife and you my man and I have a friend, if I am lonely I got someone to pray with, talk with, go to dinner with, and to yell at, I laugh' because I had always talked to God like he was and is my best friend since I develop a relationship with him'

This was the end of 2005, I ignored the voice of God because I was so happy with my life in Jesus, I did not want anything to interfere with the love I had for God.

This male ministry was singing at this church at the time and I was walking out the door and the spirit of God spoke again saying go and give him a kiss on the check for me and let him know that I love him, and it will be okay, I said to myself lord are you okay? I will not touch that man, he would think I want him and I am okay, then the lord ask me if you love me and obey me like you say then you would trust what I am saying, I was kind of mad, but I obeyed the voice of God, I walked back into the church and walked over to the young man and gave him a hug and kissed him on the cheek and told him that God loves him and it will be okay, he looked at me with a surprise look, with a smile like he knew what I was saying was true, he said thank you, and I went on my way I

kind of laughed to myself and said lord you are off the hook'
At this time I went home and me and my mother was talking
about some things in my past, my mother never wanted to
hear about the past she would get upset and did not want to
deal with what she did or cause, so I just prayed that God
would let her know that she got to face some things before
God could release her to her future.

She was in denial, she knew it was true, but she wanted to
leave it behind without forgiving or ask for forgiveness.

So I started taking her to the church I was going to and she
loved it she started seeing the spirit of God move in people
life's, then she started getting involved and in 2006 she gave
her life to Christ. Even though she gave her life it still was
some things God needed to do in her, she still had something
in her that hinder her from loving me totally.

Well me and this man I meet in church started to communicate
more that I met, and everything was not that great in this
man all he ever did was jump from woman to woman and
he was a good man deep down inside, and we had a lot in
common, many times I had to go to God and say lord I know
you don't have this man for me' because he got too much
work that need to be done in him for me to deal with, but
we became best friends, I would talk to him a lot concerning
my struggles and he would open up to me concerning his, it
was hard to really date him, but we was good friends because
of his life style with too many other women that would put
a red flag up, but I would always encourage him to read his
word and let God love him the way he need to be love, we
really had a lot in common, his loneliness and wanted to be
love and someone to love him,

I remember when I felt that way, our back ground was kind of the same but he was raised with his parent and he was not abused, but he did feel not supported to become success in his life, but I would encourage him with my testimony to let him know it was never too late for God to change and arrange him in what God is calling him to be. A Godly man first. This man had a good heart deep down inside, it was just all over the place.

But for some reason God connected us together, I just did not see my self-being his wife, at least at that time. But we enjoyed each other company, well now It is 2007 and my mother is still holding on, still fighting this sickness she has in and out of hospitals and nursing home, I prayed every day that God would bless her, we started spending more time like a mother and daughter should, I loved my mother, we had some ups and down but our relationship became stronger, even with all her the hurt she afflicted me with, I found myself loving her through it all.

I had a great help in dealing with what I was going through, a mother of the church that had twelve boys told me one day "no matter what we go through or what people have done to us we got to have a different approach", we got to still give love as children of God, we only would have "one mother" that God has given no matter how many play a role as a mother God gave us our parents to respect and if we obey the word of God we will see the true blessing in that. It made me think that no matter what happen I got through because of the seed God implant within me, and maybe something happened in my mother past that cost her traumas that intervene in caring for me and my brother, and some generational curses are to be broken and not mended back together, my mother started being a friend to me even with the hidden backstabbing at this time, I really did not care I just wanted to love her and forgive her and be the daughter she needed me to be. I really would not understand her pain, only God! I don't know what she has been through.

But I was here for her in case she wanted to open up, I just wanted her to know that she was forgiven and I loved her no matter what.

So this brother and I relationship got serious, he was singing for God and I was called to preach and teach his word, we became closer as time went by, he helped me a lot in caring for my mother, but there was always some type of issue he had, woman! Because I was saving myself for God right time in for my life, he did not totally understand that because of the women he dated allowed him to stay and live and sleep with them, and these women were in church like I was, but as time went by I explain to him some of my past so he could understand, I gave him scriptures to look up so he would understand about the temple of God, I hated to see him in this type of web that the devil was holding him in, so I prayed for his deliverance, I asked God why the man I was friends with for four years never tried or ask to touch me and we spent lots and more time together than the man you say would be my husband?

One preaches the word and the other sang the word?

But as time went by I understood that the enemy had deceived him so many times and all he ever wanted was to be love and God was the one that was going to give it to him and I needed to be patient and see the salvation of God move.

Sometime we give up on people before God tells us to, and a lot of us miss out on our true blessings.

The crazy thing about being with him, was that it would hurt him to even hear that I went through the things I went through, and his heart was so much in making me happy, pleasing me, talking to me like the lord would have some do, but I rejected it a lot because of his short comings of wanting me to love him not only mentally but physically, and I was not going to take it to that level,

But we remained good friends through it all,

I was always was in and out of town working for the lord, to tell you the truth I never had a man that shared tears with me and cared that much about what happen to me even my friend from church did not do that, so I knew he had some form of heart God in him,

He just did not know how to really let go and let God work it out for him, he did not know about the Holy Spirit that comes in and live in you, the power he needed to change some things in him. No one ever took the time to explain or teach him what the word of God says about this type of activity. So the devil knew his weakness and tried to destroy him with it, but we know God is always on time.

Well it is 2007 still hanging in there with mom and this new love I got in my life but still depending on God for what I need and want, ministry was strong it had its ups and down, but we know that everyone that call On the name can also be full of game,

The lord was using me in ways I never could of imagine, my life testimony helped a lot of people and the relationships, what I had with my mom, helped delivered other daughters and mothers.

At this time I was going through a lot because my mother health had truly turned to the worst, her health had put her in intensive care and I was so busy running back and forth to the hospital, not knowing but holding on to faith that God would pull her through, I needed a little more time with my mother, It still was things I needed to talk to her about, and at this time I did get a little weak in my walk with God, my man friend was going through some things so we feed off each other strength, I allowed him to move in to help him out for awhile at this time, I felt that I was doing the right thing, I hated to see anyone in need, like I used to be, and if I had it I would share to the world no matter who it was.

But my spirit was warning me and I just did not believe I would fall into temptation.

I felted strong enough in the lord to sustain myself from any temptation, so I thought'

But who were I fooling we were sharing too much time together, then the kissing came from time to time, then the hugging and the love taps, lord help me please! I never felt the feelings I felt with him, I thought we would be safe as long as I kept on praying, finally I could not contain myself, he started telling me that he wanted to spend the rest of his life with me and he needed a woman like me, and I remember that God said that this man was going to be my husband, and I just let all the guards I had down, I never had a man that stayed home at night cooked, cleaned ran my bath water, loved kids, listened to me,

I just thought well lord forgive me even though the love making was good, but what happen to God commandments, I felt like I just died, I never wanted to let God down again, I really wanted to make it until the time was right.

Chapter 11

"Married with Angry Tears!

I did not save myself for my husband. I was celibate for seven years! Never been touched by anyone, I felt that I was heading for a disaster. So I cried out to God to please forgive me, I wanted to be different for once in my life, I felt guilty, I felt dirty, then I punished myself, asking myself how can I allow myself to fall so short of your glory? Was I really weak? Was I really in the will of God? Was I really your chosen vessel lord? How did I allow myself to give in so easily?

How could I listen to the enemy and let him trick me? The list went on and on.

I wanted my man friend to know that I was special and not like the other women he has been with saved or unsaved, would he look at me the same? Or as the other women he had before? How could or would he treat me different from them? We had something special and I messed it all up! I was the stronger vessel, how could I fall Lord?

This was all I thought about, I let God down, myself down, my man friend down, I had let too much of myself out and gave to soon, But he did not leave, he wanted to work it out, he wanted me to teach him how to love me, but only God could do that, So after the fall I prayed and talk with God to help us both get it right, he made me feel so safe like no man could ever do, he stayed until we got married June 14, 2008

Believe me the devil tried us both up to that day, to separate us, my mind was playing tricks on me all the time, had me believing it was not to be, but I held on to what God said and did not care what everyone else thought, it was so sad that everyone else knows what is good for you, but not for themselves, at times I thought that he was not for me because of the arguing and other people in our life's, but I took a long hard look at what was going on, and talked to God, I knew that he was not ready to be a husband yet, because God was not done with him, not that he was not my husband,

The lord let me know that in the beginning we just jumped before our season, but it would be okay if we just and believe that he could turn it around for us instead of blaming one another, we needed to come together and allow God to bring the season to us, by reading our word together, praying together, going to church together, fellowshipping ourselves with other couples that are growing together, take our relation to God not people, hold each other up when one fall, and look at our own faults instead of blaming one another, and allow God to be the leader, the middle, and the end of our marriage.

We might have got married for all the wrong reason, but I rather marry than to burn the I had always kept and remember these words from the church I was hurt in no matter how much they twisted the word of God some did make sense if the knowledge came from God word tells us in Corinthians: chapter 7 verse 9 tells us if they cannot contain, let them marry, for it is better to Marry than to burn, when I gave myself to a man, it made me feel that I gave the my most precious thing that God had for me to preserve, and I let him down, it is so sad how we allow ourselves to be caught up in this judgmental world of what people would think of us, or look down on us, I allow myself to be caught up with this title I had trying not to let anyone know that I made a mistake, but God knew, and that was all I needed to worry about not man judgment on my life, but to tell you the truth I am happy being married looking for the end of what God have for us, just the guilt was eating me up,

And keeping me from totally given in to my husband and looking at all the faults he had before we got married, It was nothing new that he did or said, I just let myself be caught up with the rumors of what people thought of him, or his past, but everything he did I knew before I married him, so now I am putting this marriage before God and waiting on his change and movement in changing him and me, but the more I had put my marriage before God the more the enemy fought against it, it had got so bad with my mother playing a part, jealous people playing a part, I started to change, I started losing who I was in God.

My drive I had for God, I lost my peace I had with God, I lost my passion for the ministry God had in me, I starting loosing the most important thing my relationship with God, it seemed like my past was knocking at the door and it seemed like it had keys to come in to take my mind, I knew that the devil is a liar,

I knew that my marriage was not a joke, it was God that spoke to me to let me know, it was me that did not wait on the right time, I was so angry of being the strong one in the marriage, I wanted my husband to take control for once but I was too scared to give him that chance, so I hid the pain again until it ate like cancer, my whole house hold was in chaos and I needed God to take control at this time, I really did not trust the women or men in the church for advice because of what they would tell me, they would say that man is not your husband, because of his action, but never offered to help him to understand what was at stack! At this time I knew my husband was not strong spiritually but he was Gods child and he just needed a male model in the spiritual family to lead him in the right direction, not for them to throw stones and bury him, so I started taking my scream I had inside out on him, not that he did not deserve it some of the times.

But it was not my battle to fight it was the lord, one day I screamed at God and told him I need you now!

If nothing else change around me then change me, Not that I deserve anything because of my disobedience, but because lord I need you now this is too big for me to handle, and then I gave him my whole marriage.

As time went by it became 2009 and my mother had to go back to the hospital, I was so drained and tiered I just could not move another step my marriage was messed up, the devil seemed to be winning at this point, and I just did not care if, I would live to see it through another day.

I know you say to yourself how can I be messed up living with God, I said the same thing to myself time &time again, they reason why I felt like this is because at this point of my life I got weary, my spiritual walk got weak because I did not care to pray read or go to church, I know this sounds like De'javu all over again, this is when I realize that I allowed Satan to take charge of my life due to the problems I was having in my marriage and with seeing my mother fade away in my face,

But I did realize that the devil has no new tricks, all he could and will do in your life is bring the same tricks from your past sins to you in all types of different forms, we just got to recognize the pattern, and anything else we do to our selves God always give you a sign on when, where and how your destruction will come, if you pay attention, we just got to stop and truly listen and stop wanting to please the flesh all the time, if you was training for a job you would follow instructions and finish the probation period, If you meet a new woman or man you was dating you would put on everything positive to make sure that this person would like you,

If you was meeting the president for the very first time how would our approach be? Then all the preparations that you would do for worldly things then what would you do for the lord? And how would you follow the instructions when the lord tells you?

If only we would stop, listen, relate, pay attention and follow the voice of the lord, a lot of turmoil we go through would not be so bad, we would see the victory at every end of the tunnel.

When I started getting tired, of being tired, of being just too tired, this is when I straighten myself up and said to myself girl you got what it takes, God has brought you too far for you to keep going in circles, when are you going to pay attention and go straight, I was My own worst enemy, because every time that I would fall I would look back and reach into my own past that the lord had deliver me from.

It was only there to remind me of how I made it through, it was only there for me to testify about, and to glorify the lord of how good he is to me, it was only there for me to know that I am his chosen vessel, but I kept on reaching for it to be a covering, an excuse for me to through my own pity parties all over again, I was stopping myself from a lot of doors opening and closing, I had my hand in the situation more than God, the lord did not set me up to fail, but to succeed the entire plan he had for me and that was to prosper and not fail,

We got to stop planning where we are going in God and just follow the plan in the order that is already ordain for our life, we get of focus too much because of self, we always want things, people and places faster than God has for us.

Something's are like playing hot potatoes, it is too hot to handle at that time and God wants to cool it down for us to handle, but we always in a rush and without patience, in his word Jeremiah he say this, for I know the Plans I have for you,

Declares the Lord' Plans to Prosper you and not to Harm you, Plans to give you Hope and a Future, and in Isaiah 40 verse 31, But they that wait on the lord shall Renew their strength; they shall mount up with wings as eagles; they shall run and not be weary; and they shall walk and not faint.

Now tell me if we believe that he died for us, so that we can live, then why is it so hard to know that God has it all covered?

Because it was all a "Set Up" for his plan to work, that he already had just for us, yes we can shed our tears but know that in Psalm chapter 30 verse 5 the lord speaks about his anger only endures but a moment in his favor is life so our weeping may endue for a night, but joy comes in the morning,

I have falling so many times with my walk with my faith, my joy, my peace, my happiness, my hope, my plan, my purpose, and my belief, but when I thought about the goodness of Jesus and all that he has done for me I said girl you are tripping, get up, pick back up that cross, and start the walking all over again, you are a solider of the most high God, and what you have and is going through is only a test of your faith'

You are more than a conquer though Christ that love you, and I shall live and not die. Said the lord!

I had to get myself back in order, no matter what was going on all around me, my marriage was falling apart, my kids were acting like fools, my spiritual family was lacking in encouraging me, so I had to encourage myself, by reading my word, fasting and praying and having hope that my change was on the way.

Now it had come that my mom was leaving me, we still have not resolved all my answers, I still was puzzled to know if she truly loved me or not, but I thank God for the time of having her in my life, we had built some type of relationship' some was good and some was bad, but tell me who has a perfect relationship?

I got what I needed and that was my mother again, to hold and kiss her, and to tell her that I loved her, not only that but to show her that in spite of what, how, or who said what, God had done this thing, and he was in charge.

I was able to let go and let God heal a broken piece in me that I never had fix and that was time with my mother, and to truly forgive her, my mother past away to be with the lord on July the 3 2009, I never knew that it was going to be that hard to let go, because we only had a little time together but I know that I had the time and I had to give God thanks for that, I felt like a part of me was gone, I felt so bad for my baby sister because she was in prison when our mother past away, and I wanted to be there for her, and I couldn't, I knew that she depend on my mother for everything and it was going to be hard for her to let go.

As time went by I started blaming myself for not having my mother in my home at the time she died, she had gotten so sick that it was so hard for me alone to care for her, and I had so much going on in my marriage, that I did not want her to suffer no more than she already was,

Chapter 12

"I Still Need Her!

I picked her up one day from the nursing home, she had been in there 2 weeks, and for some reason I felt that me and her needed to have lunch together, and spend this day together, so I brought her back home and fix lunch for us both, and we had the best time we ever had through my whole life together, she had told me that she knew that I had been through a lot, and that she was so sorry that I went through all that pain, she open up to me about some things that had happened to her in her child hood of her being raped and beating, and her street life, tears were in my eyes to know I finally got the answer I needed my mother had gone through some pain like I had and no one helped her or loved her the way she needed to be loved, until she came here and received Christ in her life, She thanked me for everything I did and told me she was sorry and really want me to be happy, she could not eat the lunch I fix, and became very tired, and wanted to go back to the nursing home and lay down, but she still could not say she loved me, I said to myself maybe one day'

But I never knew that it was our last supper together, he next day I got a call that my mother was not Responding and they were sending her to the hospital, when I got there she was not looking good, I was so full of pain and really had no one there for me but God, so I cried out to the lord asking him to please take her pain away, let her not suffer any more, no matter what it cost me, give her rest, I came home and told my husband after I got out the shower before I was going back to the hospital that God was going to take my mother, I went back to the hospital the doctors let me know that she was not doing good, and that they were not able to get her mediation in her, so the last two days I had with her was just me letting her know that I love her and forgive her, as I laid in the bed with her and holding her hand I told her that I would be okay, and she can rest with God now, with tears in my eyes I did not want to let go now we just started talking to one another and opening up to one another, I felt that I needed more time with her,

But I needed to let go and let God do what he needed to do for her sake, my mother was an energizer bunny always on the go and shopping and doing her favorite dance. She opened her eyes for a minute and called my name, as I was standing she called with a loud voice, I will never forget the loud sound she made, like she wants me to be okay and did not want to leave me again, until I was okay' but I let her know that I was okay, and that God had me.

I told her that I will and shall be happy, and that she can let go now, I gave her a kiss' and told her I would be right back, I went home and asked my husband to come to the hospital with me because my mom was not doing well, and I need someone with me, I truly knew that this was it and I was going to say good bye to my Mom.

I was gone for only 15 to 20 minutes, when I walked in her room I seen a tear in her eye, and walked toward her, at that second she looked at me walking in the hospital room, and then when I got closer to her she stop breathing, she had waited on me to return before she let go and went with God,

It hurt more than I ever could ever imagine, then my mother phone rang and it was my baby sister on the phone and I had to let her know that our mother just past, it was the worst news I ever had to give my sister, knowing that I had called the prison to tell them my mother condition, and my mom was waiting on that call from her baby, that was the worst news I wanted to give her while she was locked up, all I could do is say lord help her and give her strength, As I was dealing with all this' my heart was so heavy no one around me really truly knew what I was feeling because all they knew was my mother never raised me, so it should not be hard.

But they really did not and cannot understand the deep hidden love I had for my mother, a love that God planted and no matter what people thought and seen, she was my mother, and I loved her, this was why I was so hard on myself because my mother never wanted to go in a nursing home, but at the last days I had to, I was going through too much I wanted to leave my marriage, things were not good at all, so I started to blame myself for her dying early,

So as I was planning the homecoming service for my mother I was sitting in my chair with tears in my eyes wondering lord I don't know how I am going to pay for my mother funeral her insurance was not much, I just got it when she moved from New York and I had to have it over two years and it was only 19 months that I had it, so I was crying and I heard a voice call out my name, it was so plain that everyone in the house could of heard it, so I got up walked to my bedroom and asked my husband did he call me, he said no, so I went back and sat In the chair and the voice called me again, I said to my husband I know you called me, and he responded you are tripping, I did not call you then I said to myself girl you are tripping, you better call on Jesus, I looked at my mother's picture and said ok mom what are we going to do? Letting her know that I was sorry for putting her in the nursing home, I told her that I was sorry for not being able to care for her myself and keep her home with me because of all the arguing,

I did not want her to get sick anymore and I was sorry for her seeing me act a fool, every now and then, being a woman of God I should have had better control, even through me and you had our ups and down I needed you to stay focus on God so he could heal your body, I was talking to her picture like I she was standing there herself in the flesh.

I was so angry with my husband for not helping the situation get better, I was mad that he was not a strong vessel at the time of my weakness, I felt like I was in this marriage alone and fighting for a lost battle.

At that moment I felt a calm hand go across my face I looked around to see if anyone touched me, that Touch was a mother touch, I know that touch' it felt like that the touch that my mother gave me on my wedding day, at the moment I could not stop crying, I knew that my mother heard me and knew that I loved her and she was watching over me, And that she was okay, it was just too hard to say goodbye for now.

Now it was two weeks after my mother was gone I was going through some personal feelings inside and I needed God's to help me understand something's, maybe I was not reaching out to God enough, being so weak, my church family did not check on me since the funeral,

And that was so sad when you think you got the people of God to help you through a difficult time, it was no one around, so I took out some of the personal pain I was feeling on my husband, because of what I had went through with him, the things he had done and allowed the enemy to step in and direct him in a mess up state of mind, I was mad that he did not feel the pain I was feeling, and the abandonment I was feeling, so instead of forgiving and working it out I wanted to push him further away from me, I slow down in doing the women ministry, it seemed like all it was doing was sucking more life out of me, I let go of the children ministry, I did not have enough drive to push myself to gather them together,

I was tired of going to church with the same old testimonies and songs, and people acting like they cared, because I never received a card or call, or not even a knock on the door, so I separated myself, from forms of things, but not God, I loved the lord no matter what I was feeling, I knew without a shadow of any doubt he loved me and cared for me,

I talk to the lord daily, one day I was driving my car and heard the lord voices asking me why have you looked for others to wipe your angry tears away'

Why are you looking in all the wrong places? I am here with you, I will give you the strength you need just ask, you are forgiven, forgive yourself, you are loved, so love yourself, I Have set you free from all the fruit from the bad tree, I have planted a new seed in you that wants to bare the good fruit that I have being watering in you, the branches are growing but the weeds that you picked up are in the way of keeping the good fruit from blooming, just step aside and let me finish the good work I have started in you.

Chapter 13

"She Really Loved Me!

And when I stepped aside and let go and let God, he started plucking the weeds, and now I was feeling my fruit grow!

The tears that I have been shedding night and day since my youth has build me a harvest that is waiting for me, this is when I received that key to endure the angry tears I was shedding through my walk with God, I had receive the power to stand through any test that has and is coming my way. I am God's anointed, I am chosen, Glory be to God, when I was able to stop my car I jumped out and did a victory dance it was like fire shut up in my bones, I felt like David in the bible, I danced so hard my clothes almost came off, I was finally free from my own self destruction' do this mean I am perfect? and will not go through anything else? Or that my trials and tribulations were over? No it means to me that I am who God says I am, I belong to him, and I will make it, no matter what storms, winds, floods, hurricanes, tornadoes, come my way as long as I got king Jesus I can make it, and believe me the devil is not done,

I am a threat to his mess, for one I love the lord, second I got the lord in me, third I am obeying the lord word, fourth I am following the lord, fifth I got a made up mind, six I have gotten back up from the traps he set for me to fall in, and seven I got the power to resist him when he appears.

One day I was at home and going through some things of my mothers, looking and throwing all her paper work that I did not need, and packing her clothes to donate and give some to my sister and my grandmother and saving something's for my baby sister, and I run across a tablet, I open it up and it was a journal, that my mother was keeping, it was her last words by looking at the date before she went back in the hospital for the last time, I never knew she was writing, and it was all about me, how she loved me, how I was her angel, how she was so proud of me, how she thank God for having me, and how she was so proud and happy that she was with me in her last days, and how much she really loved me, it was so touching' I cried through reading it all,

I had my answer, all these years of wondering, begging, praying for the words of my mother saying that she loved me' Thank you Lord' my Mother really did love me, and never wanted to give me away, she was trapped by the enemy games just like I was, and was glad that I was the one who rescued her, she told me why and how she was abused and felt not loved, and how she ended up in the mind set she was in, she never knew how to care or love us, she was lost herself, and survived the best way she knew how' wow reading what my mom went through, I knew and understood her pain and angry tears, Thank you Jesus I have peace.

Now it is September 2009 I am at home and my phone rings, I get a call that my Son is very ill' and I need to get up to the hospital, this is two months after losing my mother, I was caught off guard because we just buried my mother and my husband nephew got shout a few months back multiple times, and almost lost his life,

So we were very busy in 2009 things were coming back to back, but thank God for his grace and mercy.

So I got up out of my bed rushed to the hospital, and there it was' another attack from the enemy to take me off course of what I just got delivered from, yes I was scared, yes I was hurt, yes I screamed, and yes I cried, I am still human and God gave me this heart, all I was getting from the doctors were your son is very critical' and he will not make it through the night, he has an infection that went through his whole body and into his heart that broke pieces of his heart that went into his brain that caused him three massive strokes, and if we do surgery or cut on him now he will die'

All I could do is take a deep breath, and did my motherly cry and scream but I did not panic, and then shook myself and said okay that enough now',

I looked up to God and said I am here again and you know what I am going through, you knew before it ever happened, so tell me lord' and only you tell me the real deal, I had a long talk with you lord and you told me if I step aside and let you be the lord you need to be in my life, then you would care for my every need and some of my wants, now lord I want you to fix this,

I needed you to strengthen me and carry me through whatever you got planned for my child because this situation is to deep and close to my heart, and it is a heavy load that I cannot bear to carry, heal my son right now lord, raise him up lord like you did me lord, I know your miracles lord! When you raised Lazarus up lord, how you healed the blind to see and the deaf to hear, how you made the woman with the issue of blood whole, now do it for my son lord, in the name of Jesus, this was the first step I took to allow God to wipe angry tears away, not my husband, not my pastor, not my daughter, not my son, not my friends, but you God.

This is when I saw some weeds moving that was stopping my victory, and when I allowed myself to depend totally on God and trust him at his word, he told me first that my son was going to be okay, and then he sent a pastor that told me everything was going to be okay, and the another pastor I had my confirmation that was the Father the Son and the Holy Ghost that confirmed that my son will live and not die! With a new clean heart.

Thank you Jesus you are bad all by yourself, my husband was not there by my side, I was upset that he was not holding me through this time, that was very trying, but I thank God he was not because this help me depend on God totally, this was my test of faith, to see how I was going to deal with this, even my daughter could not make it here, she had relocated and was living in Atlanta, and my baby boy was overseas and no one was able to be here for me at that moment, it seemed like God moved everyone so that I could show him that I truly believed him at his word' and to show me that he was and is the only one that can wipe my angry tears away!

So they did the heart surgery and replaced the heart valve in his heart, he had to be on three different antibiotics, but God is good and bad all by himself, I had separated from my husband a few times doing our marriage to be able to really hear from the lord, before I decided to walk away the marriage all together, because the enemy was having his way, because we both was not doing what we needed to do and that was pray together, read the word together, hold each other up, and resist all temptations, I could blame him, and he could blame me, but all in all we should of look at ourselves, I had no excuse.

Everyone around me was trying to tell me what was best for me, and what God said, this is what happens when you let people into your marriage instead of God. The only middleman that can fix any problems is God himself, anything or anyone else will tear it apart.

So this last time that we split up was a good one God spoke to us both, I confessed my faults to the lord and admitted to myself that Rome never was built in a day, and it takes patience for God to move,

I know without a shadow of a doubt that this was my husband, we were brought together for a reason, but we rushed our season, so we got to wait until the hand of God clock reach the time we rushed.

you see you can mess up your own destiny by allowing the flesh to go before the spirit like I did, but you got to recognize the mistake and stop blaming everything and everyone else, It does seems to be easy to point the blame, but when we truly stop, look and evaluate the problem and see where the sin truly came in I had to admit I let sin in before the blessing,

I allowed dedication before education, the call we both had was perfect in God eyes but we allowed the lack of the our knowledge come before the change, we knew each other in the flesh but not in the spirit, we both had the right key but it was not molded yet to fit in the right lock, we had use our spiritual walk unwisely, but I am ready do what I need to do to get it right, there is a firm foundation that the lord has for us to stand on and the enemy has a quick sand for us to sink in. and no matter how God shows, tells or warns us, we just got to have it our way,

The lord is not a restaurant that you can order only what you like'

You got to eat the whole meal when God prepares something for you, and that was what we were lacking someone forgot the vegetables and someone just eat the meat, nevertheless we both jumped to the desert.

It is funny how we always want to follow our plan, and then when it don't work we look at God like he never played the movie for us, he gave it to us for free, but we just had to go pay for someone else copy. And we never pay attention on what he really had on the inside, to see how much it really was going to cost us.

Me and my husband was separated three times never stayed away to long, but long enough to see that we did this, no one forced us, we agreed before God to do this no matter if it was now or later, so now we got a little more struggles to endure, long as we let go and let God show us his way, his plan, his wisdom and knowledge we would be able to understand why we got to go through to receive.

Chapter 14

"Standing Still!

Now we are together holding on to see what God had in the beginning, when we stop looking through other people eyes, that looks and seem bad, but look through Gods eyes and see the hidden treasures, then we know without a shadow of any doubt that God has called for this to be, we just did it before his time, and before he finished what he started in us, so now we got to just wait, go through, hold on, stand, on the promises of the lord will for us, Thank you Jesus I can't wait to see the results.

For example "take a cake when you bake it, do you share it before it gets done? Or do you wait until it is finished and cool off, before you cut a piece? That's like God he wants to finish the project enough to present it to us, and that way when a piece falls, it would not be difficult to pick it up and place it back in the right place, allow whatever you do for God be of good timing and in the right season' before you drive off, stop when the light is red, yield when the caution light is flashing and go when it turns green.

No I am not finished, and yes my marriage will and is a working process, but when God gets finish then we know it is time to leave this earth because no marriage is perfect and will be in a working perfection as long as we are in this flesh.

No matter what it is that you have or doing with God, never give up until God say so, because everything that serves God is a working process and will not be totally finish until he comes back for us, if someone tells you that they are or they have an perfect marriage, they lied' but you will and could see good results, I have and will have things that are going to come my way to test me on every hand as long as I serve King Jesus, but I am ready and getting ready to move to the next level having my whole armor on, so watch out haters of the world, I am coming out and I want the world to know what God is going to show, in me, through me, and around me, so whatever the devil thought he has done, God is working it out in my favor,

Psalm 68 verse 1 says let God arise, let his enemies be scattered, let them also that hate him flee before him, as smoke is driven away, so drive them away as wax melt, before the fire, so let the wicked perish at the presence of God!

Yes It is sad that people would bet and sit around just to see what's going on in your life, always wondering what is the next moved, but when I was a little girl no one cared what was going on,

They never wanted to hear the pain, but loved to see you play the game of failure,

would follow my life when I would go left, they would follow my life when I would go right, they even followed my life when I went backwards and especially when I felled, but when I got up and went straight they would not follow any more' What a laugh. I love it!! Thank you Jesus, I asked the lord one day, lord what do you have on my life that when I walk' the ground shakes?

I thank God every day, I want to see what my ends going to be, It is not easy being chosen, being called is like walking through, but being chosen is going through, we have came too far with too much testimony to turn back now,

I don't like to test a lie, but I want to share that God is able to make it work if we put it in his hands, so I guess you are wondering if my angry tears have been wiped away yet?

No but they have been getting lighter and lighter as the trials and tribulations comes, me and my husband decided that we are not to old that God can't bless' just read Abraham and Sarah story in the bible.

We are still together, no rather it is one year or fifty years we made a vow to the lord to allow him to do what he needs to do with us, to hang on and see how the next book of my story ends, don't forget God is making us over and it takes time, Gods time and not man' If God can't do it, no one can.

I thank the lord for not letting me go, and helping me to understanding the battle that he has won on my behalf, no matter what the world throws God has a mitt that can caught all things on your behalf.

Let me share a little something with you, when I thought that it was all over for my marriage I called a divorce attorney, and paid the money, and when it was time to sign I was at the social security office and a stranger sat next to me, we sat for a while, I never had met her before in my life, then she spoke and told me that God said not to get rid of my marriage, he was going to work it out, I was mad but for a moment due to everything I had went through with my husband, but glad that I obeyed the lord even when the tear I had was too big for me, God sent an angel unaware to wipe that angry tear, so now I know that it is not over until the lord has spoken.

Sometimes we need to encourage ourselves, in the word of God and know that God is still on the throne of his promise, through the good and the bad, know that the battle is already Won through Jesus Christ, this is my Christmas gift to the lord' the sacrifice of letting go of the past by sharing my story to the world, it is December 2009 and I am still holding on to the promises of God, no it is still a battle, and still a walk I got to go, but I know now that whatever I go through at this point God got it, if I would give it to him, I have a choice to walk the way he is guiding me or follow someone else, or do it myself, it is up to me, if I want to stay a winner by doing what's right, humble myself under subjection to the holy spirit of God, I can allow the lord to take me to heaven, or I can put myself in hell!

I truly thank the lord for giving me the courage and strength to come out the hidden closet, and take the mask of so I could share not only my story, but the testimony of my life story,

there will be more coming, but know I am not that little girl any more that was looking for everyone and everything to wipe my angry tears away,

I know now that when it is all over I know who is the lord of all my joy and who is going to wipe all the angry tears away, he let me know in Revelation chapter 21 verse 3 through 7, it says this and I heard a great voice out of heaven saying, Behold, the tabernacle of God is with men, and he will dwell with them. And they shall be his people, and God himself shall be with them, and be their God. And God shall wipe away all tears from their eyes; and there shall be no more death, neither sorrow, nor crying, neither shall there be any more pain: for the former things are passed away.

And he said unto me, it is done.

I am Alpha and Omega the beginning and the end, I will give unto him that is athirst of the fountain of the water of life freely. He that overcomes shall inherit all things and I will be his God, and he shall be my son.

After reading this all I could do is shout and know that the tears were temporary it was all for my good to mold me into what I need to be and become today and I still am being worked on but with a better drive to know what my outcome is going to be great, if I continue holding on to the lords word.

I am trying to reach all of God's people that are full of sorrow, pain, depression, loneliness, abuse, neglect, abandoned, and shame, to let them know that God is the tear of Joy. And his word is life! It is true, oh yes it is, just pick up his word "the Bible and read, believe and receive and look at my life' I am one of his witnesses, read all about yourself' find out who you really are' so you can know who you are' one day I heard a pastor talk about the keys to the kingdom of God, and I made a comment that the word of God the bible is my keys' to every part of my life situation to survive any attack that comes in my life.

As I started learning the word of the lord daily, I would see myself a lot in the women in the bible, The lord would show you what you need to know if you just get out of that self pity the enemy has trap you in, like myself and get the strength you need to come out of them dark deep places that no one was ever able to reach, it is so sad to be in church getting up daily every Sundays after Sunday and bible studies and lie to yourself that you learn something or you got delivered,

But still have no forgiveness toward anyone that hurt you,

or to share the real testimony that still hinds beneath that dark surface call denial and hold onto someone else deliverance, or to smile to leave and have that same frown when the doors shut without being free.

We have mothers, sisters, brothers, aunts, uncles, fathers, cousins and even friends that we don't help, because of that unforgiving deep down spirits that has not come out yet' this is hindering you from your true purpose,

The destiny God is trying to bring you to.

I hope as I share some of these women in the bible to you, that you would see yourself in them, and just shout and know that it is okay, God got your back' just let him know that you need his covering' and his deliverance, it will cost you nothing but surrender'

This book is for all of Gods children even a man yes a man.

Because in the beginning God created man and then made female from mans rib so that one day we will be able to become one in wholeness of the spirit of God that dwells in us and we will be able to touch in agreement.

Chapter 15

"Bible Same Pain & Deliverance!

These are the women in the bible God had given me that was in my childhood through my Adult hood.

1. Tamar who was violated by family member from the spirit of lust and was discarded, after being used by the enemy by the grief of the shame and no one wanting to believe as a child, so we felt no escape of the violence we began hatred into our hearts because no one done nothing to help, so here it is a lifelong emotional trauma, so here we are feeling like Tamar the fear, the pain, the shame of being raped and violated by someone you trust.

2. Hagar: the spirit of being rejected, abandoned and low self esteem Satan would make you feel that you are in danger to yourself he would try to destroy you before you know your purpose, even before you find the destiny that the lord has plan for you making you feel that you are bad person, never going to be nothing no one want you,

You have no right to the tree of life, and that you never going to be anything thing because no one would love you because you are surrogate mother,

3. Beersheba: a woman of beauty only by body being married and having lust after another man, desire of the flesh, and trick by the devil that would cause death and the enemy set up a death trap for someone you love allowing Satan to damage the good before God could work it out for us.

4. Women with the Issue of Blood: she had suffered for twelve long years with a disease of the issues of blood no one wanted her to touch them all her procession and money was spent on doctors that made her to believe that she was dome until she heard about a man name Jesus that would and could heal her and make her whole so she pushed her way through and got her healing and that is what some of us need to do push our way through no matter what anyone say the doctors, the lawyers,

   Our friends, family members, or our enemies we got someone that can heal all issues of life and the blood is what he healed us with.

5. Samaritan Women a social outcast: it was about her having to many husbands and the one that she had was not her own and this made her an outcast someone with an embarrassing situation with different men in her life that people would only talk about instead help and teach her the right way.

6. Leah: the unwanted wife a person that was given and not chosen out of age and duty she had to grow out of duty.

   Become someone wife that wanted someone else. So his love for was not real in the beginning

7. Now a person that we all need and wanted to be label as a Virtuous Woman: a woman that everyone could be proud of, a rare woman that first fear and reverenced God and righteousness a crown to her husband and far more than rubies to her children all would be proud of. In these seven characters that God let me learn about, I have seen myself as having and developing the same things, the same spirit person all in me, so allow me to go through all of them again, only the name of the character is was I!

1. I was violated by my family members, I was made to be a piece of flesh for them to do whatever and when even they wanted to use me, I was discarded after the enemy had his way, by the grief of shame that this happened no one ever believing me as a child, I felt no escape, this had me developing more hatred in my heart because not having a mother to talk to about this, and if I had someone would they done anything? It was a lifelong emotional trauma for me, and I felt just like Tamar full of fear, pain, and shame, of being molested by someone you are suppose to trust. But the lord has shown me the love, understanding, and compassion God shown me that he was all the comfort I ever needed,
To start my healing, he taught me how to forgive myself and others, in Psalms chapter twenty seven verse ten when my mother and father forsake me, then the lord will take me up. And in Isaiah chapter forty one verse ten, eleven, and thirteen it says fear not for I am with you, be not dismayed, for I am you God; I will strengthen you, I will help you, I will lift you with my righteousness. Behold, all that are incensed against me shall be ashamed and

confounded for the lord my God will hold me saying fear not: and believe me the lord is helping me every day of my life by guarding my heart and my mind by keeping it in perfect peace.

2. I was feeling rejected and feeling abandoned by everyone I ever came in contact with, I allow Satan to make me believe that my plan for my life was always going to be danger, I felt that if I reached out I would be destroyed even if I tried. I never felt that I had a destiny but failure, so he planted surrogates mothers in my life to make be believe I would never know a love from my real natural mother, I felt like I was a bad person, and never going to be anything in life, by being a foster child that made me have low self esteem, the enemy tried to make me feel that I had no rights to the tree of life. But the lord let me know that I was precious and wanted if I would just allow him to come in and give me what was missing in my life, and live again, he let me know that I was born again, a new creature and I would be rejected for righteousness and his name sake.

3. I felt like my body was my only beauty, the lust of the flesh was all I had to give, I was married and living with another man, because of me never hear that I was beautiful I allowed the words from men to lead me in a death situation, he lust of the eyes can be a trick to your destiny, beauty is what God has created and not what man made, we need to watch out for the sweet talkers dressed in sheep clothing, know that we need to be a bride for Jesus before we can be wife or husbands for others. Know that God has the keys to repair and restore,

confession is good for the soul, Psalm chapter fifty one verse one and two, have mercy upon me, O God according to thy loving kindness; according unto the multitude of thy tender mercies blot out my transgressions wash me thoroughly from mine iniquity, and cleanse me from sins and one John chapter verse eight and nine if we say that we have no sin, we deceive ourselves, and the truth is not in us, if we confess our sins, he is faithful and just to forgive us of our sins,

After reading my story you know that I have suffered many issues that held me from being washed in the Blood of Jesus Christ, just being afflicted with all that man said I had, I truly thank the lord for the faith That he had build up in me, when everything had me feeling like I was dome God gave me hope, everything that the enemy was and is bringing my way he had to get permission from God to even attack, but as long as I hold onto the hem of his garment the word I will and shall be made whole in the lord, in Matthew chapter nine verse twenty one and twenty two, let me know that if I would just touch the hem of his garment and believe that he is who he say he is by faith it would make be whole again, so matter what people think or say concerning my life I know that if I keep on pushing my way through the mess, the chaos, the backbiting, the lies, the closet doors,

Things might look bad and it seen like you will not make it in Matthew chapter 17 verse 20 tells us a grain of a mustard seed of faith, we can move the mountains in our life and know that we walk by faith and not by sight.

4. I have made so many mistake in my life and still
   today and tomorrow I will make them, and their
   there will be saints that really are aint's that will try to
   keep you down by them mistakes, but keep getting
   up, try your best, give God your reasonable service,
   by dieing to the flesh daily, you would always be a
   outcast to them that don't understand the calling
   on your life, it hard for you to understand but the
   battle is not with your brothers or sisters or yourself,
   it got nothing to do with us, it was all about Jesus'
   so keep your head up,
   I had to tell myself over and over again that I am
   just a vessel being use by God that is awesome all
   by itself.
   There will be haters wondering why and how you
   walked out that fire you were just thrown in, how
   did God give her or him another and another and
   another chance, why is because I got up and carry
   the cross that was meant for me,
   Then wipe the dust off your shoulders and keep
   on walking.
   I am still drinking from the fountain of life, His
   cup, the word, my life.

5. . No matter how hard I tried to please the man in
   my life rather he was a friend or my husband, if
   they were not a man from God, than you would
   still be trying to please the flesh, they would always
   want something to keep pleasing them flesh is never
   satisfy, so if you can't please God! Then why try
   pleasing Man? The eyes of the flesh seeks all that
   would keep it please, no matter how much I tried
   to be a model wife my buttons always got stuck
   and then I was cast aside but no matter how much

your button breaks or stick God got the right tool to make it work so now I put all my love and energy in the lord to mold me into what he wants me to be, you cannot give what you can't give to God, Exodus Chapter twenty verse three tells us not to bow down to men or serve them for God is our God and a Jealous God so how can we worship man more than our creator? I was Leah a unwanted wife because I allowed others to seek out the person for me and God did chose that husband for me, that is what we do today we allow someone else to tell us that is our husbands or we go out seeking ourselves, when in Proverbs chapter eighteen verse twenty two tells us whosoever finds a wife finds a good thing, and obtain favor of the lord God will send the husband in good timing his time so that we would receive the love, support, devotion, compassion, we need to become a wanted wife.

Last and the best that I am still striving for to become for my lord and Savior Jesus Christ and to my Husband, and myself is a **"Virtuous Woman,"** A person that is hard to find a woman that totally fears the lord, she Takes her relationship and responsibilities wisely, she would seek the kingdom of God and all his righteousness, I Have a drive and compassion to my family, friends and enemies to do good toward them, I love to use my gifts he Has given me and to allow the beauty I have inside to shine, a value of a virtuous woman is far beyond rubies, Now this is what I see and press toward to before the day the lord calls me home to rest, so that I can receive my

Flowers while I am still in the land of living,

1. God can trust a virtuous woman.
2. A virtuous woman has a pattern of consistent goodness toward her God
3. A virtuous woman is willing to work for her God
4. A virtuous woman makes a healthy vessel from the inner satisfaction for her God
5. A virtuous woman makes her home in love and purity for her God that is her first desire of a heart after God.
6. A virtuous woman cares for the physical need and not slothful with the ability God gives her.
7. A virtuous woman wants to be wise in business, a hard worker and commits her excellence in God
8. A virtuous woman wants to be a prayer warrior for God
9. A virtuous woman makes good judgment of protection from her God
10. A virtuous woman cares for the poor and compassionate for the needy like her God
11. A virtuous woman plans ahead so that nothing blindside her from God
12. A virtuous woman dresses herself in a properly attired she dress herself to honor her God.
13. A virtuous woman is recognize greatly by her husband, merchant, her children, for her excellence, wisdom and kindness what a honor and responsibility God could ever give a woman today, your physical appearance only last for a season, but a Godly, virtuous woman has enduring inner beauty the world could never produce having a Godly virtue, causes everyone to know to praise how bless we are, and this is

what God is looking for in men and women today when we do it God s way, we have no need to fail at anything that God put our way.

Who can find such a woman or man? I pray that this is what God finds in me on my Judgment day.

So aloud God to rebuild you in his own image so that we will not be rottenness to you own bones, know that there is no new story under the sun that God has not known or heard, so but put it out there so that someone can be healed, set them free from the chains made from the enemy.

Part 2

Power Too Stand Thru Angry Tears!

Knowing that God is all knowing he sees, hears, and knows the test that is coming ahead.

My Story was out, and the secrets were told, things that we endue and go through' that later becomes an awesome testimony after we make a stand and come out of the hidden closets, by taking off the mask, the hidden identity of who were really are, Just knowing that the mask was off and it was time for me to show the real identity was over whelming itself, it was like I was a new me, not knowing that I was hidden by the fear of others emotions,

I had truly told the truth and nothing but the truth, It was much easier to do knowing that God had my back and has loved me through all of it,

It was such an excitement to learn that the almighty' made me who I am, and no one and nothing can change that no matter what storms that lies ahead.

I am who I am' made, shaped and formed by an awesome God, I wanted to share this wherever I go, even though I have given birth before, In a natural sense, this type of deliverance of birth was so different, I really cannot explain it, this is an experience you would haven't to go through yourself to see what I am saying, just imagine when you get the news of how it feels that you have had your first child, a baby, a bundle of joy, inside of you.

You want to share this news with everyone, God's precious creation, just going through the growth with the ultrasounds and movements of this type of feeling inside of you, then comes your due date that gets you ready for this blessed day, sometimes it comes early and sometimes it comes late, and sometimes just on the exact day that was given to you.

Pg. 225

The Power Too Stand Thru Angry Tears!

But how do we get ready for a day that truly changes our life?

A date of our deliverance of all that pain, sorrow, disappointments, depression, shame, failures, a day that only the Lord can give us, the day that Jesus took your prayers to the father on your behalf, the day it all came possible that your prayers were answered, the day you received the Power to stand through the angry tears, a date that we will not know the day, the time, or the hour, but we know that God is an on time God. He may not come when we want him, but he will be there right on Time!

Now this is an overwhelming feeling that only you experience and know how it feels, there are no difference between a natural birth, and a spiritual birth, A natural birth you feel the movements, and see the growth, you feel the sharp pains, until preparation on that delivery day, the pain come like no other pain you have ever endure, then the joy,

But a spiritual birth you feel it manifest through all that pain and growth you would endure through life ups and downs, then when your deliverance date comes it is like a joy that you never endue before

So what I am saying is sometimes you have complications doing both births, pain before gain, but when it is all said and done it both comes out with the definition word "JOY! So let me tell you, how I am really doing since my true testimony, my trials, my tribulations and my birth of my deliverance, without the sugar coats on top, well Satan was mad yes he was, he has truly lost the battle where I am concern, for him to know that he has lost and always was defeated in the beginning, and it was exposed in his face, knowing that another child of God was given the revelation and truth to be made free & whole from his false identity of me, made him more of a roaring lion without a cage, like a cobra in a loose field, seeking and snapping at whosoever he can devour' But the word of God has planted my feet to stand because I have the Victory!

My works have just begun, my resume has been released, and my identity has been made known. Romans 8:37 says that I am more than a conqueror through him that loves me, now I am persuaded that nothing, death, fame, games,

Any tricks the enemy has brought my way will not and shall not be able to separate me from the love of God' my mind has been made up and will be renewed to continue this race until the end of my last tear!

Yes I am delivered from my past, and now I have the presence in front of me, my journey has begun to live, the new true identity of who I am being made to be "I Have Been Made Free" John 8:31&32, tells us if we continue his word, then are we his disciples indeed and we shall know the truth and speak the truth and it shall make you free.

My testimony of my past is and was the truth, so I have gained my identity, his disciple, and a servant of the true and living God, and now it is time my season to go through the four corners of the world and tell of the goodness of Jesus Christ, my journey has started so who do you think has appeared in the garden again? The Serpent" shooting his venom at who ever will give an ear, so now the enemy needs to plant a word of deceit in something or someone who would give an ear against his children, as he did in the Garden of Eden.

Genesis chapter 3, when he deceive Eve by telling her that she shall not surly die, if she eat from the tree that God has forbidden her husband Adam not to eat from, Here it goes the enemy the snake, he has told the weaker vessel that if she would eat from the tree that they were forbidden from they would gain the knowledge the same as God, that they would gain the right to know about good and evil.

I read this over and over again, and after 25 years of hearing this reading this I got something new out of it every time.

Just think, God was as awesome back then as he is now. he always protects us from the whiles of the enemy, if we just obey him at his word, all God want ever wanted to do is protect Adam and Eve from knowing evil, he had set up all good for them to know, and the devil knew this, so he wait until Adam was busy, so that he could get Eve alone, so he could manipulate the weaker vessel as he does us today'

He would wait until your weaker moment of your life so he can come and attack you with all his lies, so that you can disobey the word of God.

If God has brought you out of darkness into this marvelous light then why do we need Satan to tell us different? I rather have seen God all my life, than to want to know about evil, what about you? If you know God then your eyes are already open, and this is where Adam and Eve failed, so can we learn from their mistake? I would say yes' we should of, but here is where I lacked in my walk with God, my story' well my testimony was out, and Satan had me hide this awesome testimony for so many years that I was blind to my true deliverance, how can we be ashamed of our victory?

I believed that if I came out with the truth of how God healed, saved, delivered, mold, rearranged, and covered me with his blood, instead I aloud the enemy to whisper in my ear believing that if the truth came out everyone would hate me, look down on me, and treat me worse than I ever been treated, but God stepped in to let me know that I am free, and I would be living a lie if I testify about all good,

No one would be able to be healed or set free that was around me that went through the same familiar things, the plan God had for my life were greater than I could see.

The angry tears I had cloud my vision so bad, all I could see is the fog, trails, and tribulations I would go through had the way foggy, and I seem to always lose my way, until God step in just in time, and rescue me, by specking life in me saying I shall live and not die, When the fog started to get clearer, I was able to see the road map of Jesus footsteps, the more I called that name the more my eyes seen to get brighter and light to my destiny, if we just get a closer relationship with Jesus, than we can see that the Lord uses the same trees and the same fruit, but is he does use a different season! How amazing' he just flips the script, so pluck off the tree all you want, but if the season is not right we will not see the results until the Lord reveals the time, his time.

The Power Too Stand Thru Angry Tears!

My Journey Starts'

Journey Day 1, The family secrets are revealed, but no one shares the praise of the deliverance of how good God is, no one sees the forgiveness or love, only betrayal of the hidden pain, no one is excited of the testimony that can free a lot of souls, no one thanking God of his grace and mercy, if only they can hear the real true praise in this. All they can do is hate me more and point the fingers, my first response was to call my grandmother, a woman who always taught me the importance of serving God, someone that I always looked up to, I just knew she would be proud of me, and see the Glory of God!

A granddaughter that had taken the wrong turn in life, has found her way' a granddaughter that almost destroyed her plans God had for her, finally serving and trusting and working for God full time, but all I receive was a cold word, a word that almost ran chills up my body,

But God had me all on fire that I could not even feel the chill, because I am still in the flesh it hurt for a moment, but God' the enemy wanted to destroy the Joy I felt of releasing my first book, my story, my testimony. The enemy wants me to feel guilty by trying to tell me that I messed up my relationship with my grandma, because gave birth to victory!

But because I study my word I remember the scripture, the Joy of the Lord is my strength and to fear not of the evildoer, because truly that was not my grandma speaking it was that spirit of denial, shame and blame, but I let her know that I loved her, and we go through things in life so that we may be an effective witness for the Lord, and Lord wanted me to share this awesome testimony for his Glory, Because this is how we overcome, I had someone deliverance in my belly and it was time for it to be delivered, sometimes it is too hard to get through some people so all we can do is pray and let go and let God have his way.

Never argue over what God has said or done in your life, never apologize for deliverance, healing, change or anything good in your life.

Pray for those who do not understand the Power to Stand! So as my journey continues,

Journey Day 2, I had to remember that God had prepared me in advance of what I was going to face, when God release revelation' his word it cuts like an two edge sword, I had to define denial it was just like a medical term tumor, it was a blockage someone has through the bloodstream that clog and block a bloodstream to flow through the body correctly, and sometimes it travels to the brain and becomes a tumor, and when it clears healing arise and the Victory shall be the Lords.

Journey Day 3, I was getting calls daily about how my family was disappointed with the book, my Aunts & Uncles, cousins has truly turned the other cheek, but the hardest the lack of knowledge came and the more I had to pray and fast for more strength, I was so disappointed in myself because this should have been a time of rejoice and It should of been known that it was not about me at all but about Jesus!

Journey Day 4, the Lord allowed me to remember the day the postman delivered the box the day 1, when I opened the package, how the tears overflowed with Joy, me and my husband were so excited, you would of thought we won the lottery or something, my bills were overdue, my home was in jeopardy.

I had no money, my husband was not working, all the income I had I invested in doing my first book, living on a month to month disability check, sometimes it came and sometimes it messed up, But God supply all my needs, As I followed every step the Lord was guiding me, I never went without, The more I reached the more he received me,

Journey Day 5, What' a wakeup call, I allowed the devil to make me feel guilty' the enemy had me feeling guilty of what I have done, I found myself asking the lord has I done something wrong? Even through the lord have given me instruction to write my story, so why was I feeling this way?

My flesh was trying to rise up, so it was time for my spirit to go into the battle, the spirit of God had to take complete control, the more I gave it to him to take over my mind, the more he renewed my mind with his word.

His voice spoke to me in 2 Corinthians chapter 13 verse 8 we can do nothing against the truth, but the truth that we are glad, for when we are weak we become strong, I have given you instruction to use the power I have equipped within you to edification not to destruction. So be of good comfort, be of one mind, live in peace, and the God of love and peace shall be with me.

I knew then I needed to always have the whole armor of God on, because the enemy was not going to stop, He was not going to stop trying to destroy any of God peoples, if you got a story to tell, tell it, it is the enemy job to try to stop the blood line of deliverance, your story is a testimony to make someone free, It is his job to try and attack everything and everyone that is close to your heart and that would be your love ones to throw you off the warrior line, if he can get you off guard then he feels you will stumble and fall and never get back up, so why not attack the ones that you love' he got to get to your heart the best way he can, so that you would be hinder to focus, well he tried it with me over and over again, after that would not work, the fire got turned up a little more, my finances got blocked, No money, my husband was not working. I only had one income a month, so I guess if he freeze the money I would not be able to get books to give away or sell,

I could not afford advertising, so others could hear about the book, I could not afford to travel to take the book where it needed them to go, so the fire got turned up even more, because I would not give up on sharing this testimony, my story,

I was called to speak at engagements, and this was a break through, then he decided to attack my children physical and mental, by needing my help' so every dime I would make would go on helping them.

But after my tithes were paid, no matter what I needed all I had to do is call on Jesus, and he would arrive right on time, no matter what it all belong to the lord, so after all that failed he start on my marriage, we would blame each other for what was happening to us when really it was out of our control, all we needed to do is hand it over to God and run closer and tighter, this is the time we needed to be strong for one another, we had to go back to the day the book arrive and put our hearts together as one and see the beauty of what God did,

My husband art work for the cover, my story and testimony inside, and God instructions and vision to make this book alive, so it can become a ministry of deliverance, peace, joy, forgiveness and victory, a revelation of God is still in control of miracles, to let others know that he is still in the blessing business, this is not a joke the devil is a lie.

God's word will never come back void, Isaiah chapter 55 verse 11 through 13 tells us that nothing that the Lord has spoke concerning my life shall not come back to him void, but what he has spoken in your life shall prosper, where ever the lord sends you, you will go out with Joy and be led with Peace and it shall be to the lord for his name sake, an everlasting sign that shall not be cut off.

So I am more excited knowing that this book will prosper more, so in the kingdom to make a lot of people free. What a joy to know God choose me for his Glory, as a vessel being use to help others.

What an honor, to be use by God, his word let me know to be confident of this very thing, that he which hath begun a good work in me will perform it until the day of Jesus Christ, Philippians 1-6 also let us know no matter what the Enemy tries to do to me or you know that the Battle is already won, keep your eyes ahead and watch the Lord Bring it to Past.

This is why a lot of people back up on their True Testimony' we give the enemy to much credit by allowing him to bring false statements to us'

Such as the story name "Fear" we are too busy worrying about what others think and say and the fear of losing other's out of our life's, Fear of losing someone approval over our life, Fear of what other may think, God tells us in 2nd timothy chapter 1: verse 7 & 8 for the lord has not given us the spirit of fear, But of power and love and of a sound mind, so don't be ashamed of your testimony of what you have been through and how God delivered you from out of prison the enemy locked you in,

We can share and swap stories of what happened in the bible days, but what about now' the bible we have in us, the testimonies of you and me. Let your neighbor's, brothers & sisters know about his Grace & Mercy.

It is so easy to tell someone about someone that will and can help them, but it is hard for someone to believe that Jesus would help them through whatever they are going or have been through because they cannot see the person you are talking about, so let them see the living testimony in you, that would prove that Jesus is still in the blessing business, and he will and can work it out, that would see through you of how you over came and made it through by seeing your life now, it would help them see when all hope is gone Jesus will and can step right in, but you need to prove how you did it by showing that true light of God in your walk, your talk, your faith, your belief, your lord, your testimony.

The lord has no Respect of Person' no matter what it is, we all will have to give account for our actions to the lord rather it happened today or 20 years ago, So share how the lord Grace and Mercy made you free from the hand of the enemy, witnessing is a very important part of Ministry, rather we believe it or not, How can the Blind Lead the Blind? How can you tell someone that they can make it from a storm unless you have been in one also?

It is like walking in a dark room and having someone to follow you to the Destination Point either they would walk into you or walk the wrong way without holding your hand or hearing your voice,

But with the light on they can see their way clearly, we need to be effected witnesses by sharing the whole picture and let them see how the picture manifest through you, the Road is hard but you would fall hard if you do not lean on God to carry you all the way, my burdens seemed to get heavy when I came clean and started empting my alabaster box of all my hidden secrets before the lord,

Even though God is all knowing and all seeing, we still got to confess our sins so they can be forgiven 1st John chapter 1 verse 9 and the lord wants us to cast all our cares on him, 1st Peter chapter 5 verse 7 because he cares for us!

So know that if God cares for us' then he wants the best for us, giving your true testimony is hard' but when you think of the Goodness of Jesus and all that he has done for you, where you were, where you've been, what you have done, what have been done to you, and where you are at this point. Your Soul Just Screams Out, it could of, should of, would of, been you if Jesus was not on your side.

When I think about what I have shared of my life, my testimony' I would of thought that was all but everyday that I awake with my mind stayed on Jesus, I have another Testimony, the enemy will never stop trying to set traps, but no matter what he does or make up concerning your destiny, always know that God knows the plans he has for you' in Jeremiah chapter 29 verse 11 his word speaks that the Plans to Prosper you and not to harm you Plans to give you hope and a future. This is why I will keep on running telling my testimony and sharing the goodness of the lord where ever I go, it may look cloudy and even it might look impossible but knowing that I have God on my side nothing is impossible for my lord.

My Faith has increase doing this time, you got to have Faith to see what God is doing Faith is the substance of things not seen, Hebrews chapter 11 verse 1 Serving God is a faith walk you got to know that you know that you know that god is who he say he is,

I have doubted have my life if the lord loved me or care and it drained at a lot of my energy when all I had to do is pick up the bible and read for myself and look all around me and see that if God did not care or love me I should of lost my mind a long time ago why should I feel dismayed about how my family, friends or enemies feel concerning my testimony if it don't make any since to them or they feel threaten concerning my healing, deliverance, my relationship with God,

If they are not happy that I have found Peace in God and shouting Praise instead of crying, hating, being envy, hurting myself then maybe they never knew me at all' and it is time to step aside, who can question the Power of God?

Power to make a stand through the tears!

If we just take the time to sow then we can reap what we can see, allow God to finish the growth,

In my walk with the lord I was able to feel the relationship was growing as I sowed all my affliction that I had in myself and what others has done to me I was able to recognize that I was being attack for a purpose' and all I had to do is find format and follow instruction, the format was the word of God and the instruction was my destiny.

We have a mission statement that we will make known, concerning the words "ME" "I" and until we get out of self pity parties we will not be able to see the words Plans & Purpose the plan is the me and purpose is God the "I" the Author and Finisher of our Faith Hebrews 12-2 say I can remember everything Bad that happened to me, but had to struggle to remember the good and I always wondered why and I would pray and ask God to help me remember all good and no bad, and one day I heard the Lord as I was reading my bible in Ephesians chapter 4 verses 20 thru 32 that my mind needed to be renewed daily I had to think differently, speak different,

Walk different, socialize different, and my bad situation was my good when I think about how I made it this far, I had to know that God has forgiven me and my past was going to work in my favor, my future was in God's hands, my situation has already been concluded no matter what the enemy was doing nothing and no one is Greater than my God. I could walked away from my destiny, my testimony, my ministry God has in me I was given the choice, But after I had one night with the King my lord and Savior it was no turning back. Tell your story, testify to the Glory of God, help those that are lost and release those from prison by sharing the love of Jesus through your testimony.

We pick up the newspapers, magazines to hear about bad news why? Then ask yourself why could we not pick up the bible or listen to someone testimony to hear about something good that can renew the mind?

Is very important to know the devices that the enemy can attack to destroy you' he can afflict your body, your fiancés, your family, everything around but if your mind is in the right mind set' on the things of Jesus' that type of thinking can let you know that you will make it through the trails & tribulations.

I was in a mind set of not knowing, not caring, not understand, not stable, and was with God, I was able to break through that state of being unstable, when you are in a stage of being undecided in who you are' the word of God speaks of this in James chapter 1 verse 8 a double minded man is unstable in all his ways and this is how Satan loves for us to be undecided, one foot in and one foot out, confuse, troubled, hot one day and cold another, happy one day and sad another, if he could keep our minds in this state of mind then we will never come clean and confess our sins, this type of living keeps the enemy happy and he feed off this for his strength,

He has no power so he needs to train us to boost his plan his love hate relationship, he loved us when we are following is steps and hate us when we change partners,

God loves us no matter what' unconditional, even when we are in our sins even when we turn our backs on him the lord loves us, and this is what Satan hates so he would do whatever he can to turn our life upside down, only if he could steal our minds, so this is why we need to renew our minds daily with the word of God so we can become stable, while we still have time, for every season of our life the lord has an appointed time for all things Ecclesiastes chapter 3 verse 1 thru 12 it is very easy to go around town telling everyone about how much you are saved and got Jesus in your life because you go to church every Sunday and occasional bible study, but what about sharing that true testimony on how the Power helped you stand through the angry tears, the ones that no one but God knows about, there is no new thing that God do not know, about.

Matthew chapters 10 verse 26 & 28 tells us "do not fear anyone or be scared to share your mastery of what you been through and how God brought you from, because there is nothing covered that the lord will not disclose, it will be revealed in due season so fear not those who want to hurt your body by speaking negative concerning you, but fear the one that could destroy it all both soul & body in Hell! The lord also let's us know in Mark chapter 4 verse 22 that there is nothing hid that will not be manifested and there are no secrets that should come, abroad. In Psalms 69' David shows us how when his heart was broken and sad how he could only serve to God, even in his recklessness he could not hide his sin from the lord, That it would be uncovered, this is how I felt, But thank God for his Glory his Mercy and his Grace, he has given toward me. I am at peace now more than I ever been, and we can just believe the lord at his promise and come out them dark rooms, All pictures of your life must and will be expose,

And now it is time to open up some more of yourself when we think you have done all that you need to do, here comes more thing you need to deliver.

It is like washing clothes as soon as you did all the laundry here come another load out of nowhere that you may have over looked or just said it could wait until next time, but you found out that it was one thing you needed in that pile to wear, that fits with what you are wearing, well this is how God guide us, it is something you have been through or done that he had cleaned up and washed it off, then comes this one thing you said to yourself, well maybe I will get rid of it later or deal with it at a later time, but at that moment you need to tell someone to help them through it ask yourself how could I witness to them if I am still not delivered or free from it, when you tell your testimony, no it does not mean you need to pour out all your guts at that moment, but there is a time and season for your story.

I had myself "the flesh" believe it was helping, it was lying' when I was stretching the truth a little! Sometimes we allow self to get too involve when God sends us to do a work, it does not mean you tank over, just do as the lord instructs, and then step aside, and let God handle the rest,

I could of got myself in a condition of doing 5-10 years in prison "but God" if it had not been for the lord on my side I do not know how I could of made it through.

Working in the ministry, being faithful to church, paying my tithes, reading his word, studying his word, picking up souls to come to church, working in my community faithfully, testa-lying every week. What I mean about testa-lying is I was in a make believed state of mind believing what I was doing was God's work, helping others I call it, but digging a hole deeper for my spiritual death.

I had got in so well I could not see the plot of the enemy in it, the "Sin" because the cover was helping others in need, this is what the enemy was showing me, helping in a wrong way when God gave for me to be a blessing or support to someone, I allowed my mind to be of a voice telling me it was the right thing because I was helping others, we God have you to be a blessing it will be with no lying, stealing, deceit, blame or wrong about it!

One day I was praying as I heard a message on my TV, Joyce Myers was giving It stopped me in my track, my heart started skipping a beat, I was feeling so ashamed, tears ran down my face so fast I wanted to die, I shouted out "Lord please help me, what have I done, Lord what have I done to thee, Lord how could I be so stupid, I am a woman of God how could I turn this way, how could I not see the wrong in this, what happen to me, I had so many questions concerning my transgression, as I prayed all that day and night for God to help me and forgive me,

I repented all day for what I allowed the enemy to say, mess in my ear, oh you okay, you did not do nothing wrong' it okay' God wants you to help people this way God is not upset with you, you are helping people you love, so how is that wrong?

You are doing incredible things, keep doing what you are doing, it's okay, so I did it again and also believing I was okay and God was okay with what I was doing because I was helping Gods children then as time went on I was studying the word because I had to give a speaking engagement and the lord spoke again to me in Romans 7 verse 15 thru 25 letting me know that my mind was in prison of my sin,

When I wanted to do good, evil was always there then a word on TV came forth this time a message from Joel Osteen coming from- Colossians 1-13 & 14 letting me know the Lord rescues us from a life of sin, all I had to do is acknowledge the sin, and be made available from the trick of the enemy,

I was being convicted from the evil I let myself to believe was right, but was wrong because I was breaking the commandments of God by lying to help others, stealing by thinking I was helping others by doing fraud what I mess I found myself in.

You see you really might not think a little lie is okay, or a small covering the law is okay, but that is all you need to do is a little and that is all the enemy needs to get over to win your soul to hell, all we need to do is create a crack and he will make a mounting hole that could set you up to fall right in, next you would find a false identity of who world say you are, the devil can turn you as long as you keep thinking its okay, just one more time, I had found myself in a situation that only God could pull me out!

So I tried to cover it up because now it happen again guilt of letting the people of God know I messed up, I felt I had to save this picture they painted me to be, this position of being a leader I did not want to tell anyone I knew I messed up,

Due to knowing that they would look down on me and everyone will know that I was not perfect ha, ha what a joke I was living, how could I think I was true when God tells us in Romans chapter 3 verse 23; That all have sinned and will fall short of the glory of God, In Proverbs chapter, 24 and verses16 tells us that a just man falls seven timed and rise again.

The Lord wants us to consider it all as joy when we come into the divers temptation, know that the trying of our faith, works, patience and if we lack wisdom ask God, but ask in faith without wavering.

We sometimes use all of our research and teaching in vain, what I mean by that, we listen to the Pastors and Leaders of God for what they say, but we never understand what we've learned to the Lord for him to give us more of an understanding and teach us what it really means,

Some of us get it twisted, a Title does not and will not make you who you are, or take you where you are going, We get caught up too much in the Name of the Titles and less in what the true meaning behind the title is, The Lord tells us that even the every elect will be fooled and fall, but the issue will be will you get up and ask for forgiveness?

Be Godley sorry for what you have done and do that sin no more.

I found myself going before the Lord, feeling so bad, knowing that I have fallen again, actually needing My Lord, My Daddy help hopelessly afraid of what was felt and how I had hurt him, This might sound crazy, but I was feeling good about something concerning this disorder, I allowed myself to get in a place where I did not care about what others thought of me, I had struggled with this in my past, my only concern would be that I let God down.

I was able to keep my head up through all the mess, because God had raised my shame, when I did not feel worthy to do his work the Lord kept me in such a mind frame that I could only do his will, teaching, ministering, to others while still working on the battle field for my life and for my Lord and Savior Jesus Christ.

What a powerful and merciful God I serve. I got to take time out to thank the Lord for never giving up on me, for forgiving me time after time after time and the list goes on. For raising my shame, for healing my heart, mind & soul, for keeping his hand on my life, for believing in me, for my awesome walk with the Lord.

Lord, you keep on blessing me over and over again, even though I had to lose a lot of people I truly loved, and when I hurt and betrayed the closer ones to me, even when people gave up on me, even when I tried to give up on you Lord, and believe me Satan tried his best to shut me down, Lord you stepped right in and never allowed Satan to touch my soul, now that is worth shouting out Glory! Glory!

Now let me tell you the Lord worked that situation out for me like no other would. I never went to court it was thrown out, they could not find reason to detain me to jail, Even when I told on myself, I gave all kind of information on what I have done, they just looked at me and said, "we see the evidence, and we understand what happened, and what you were trying to do, but everything is ok your records are fine do not do it anymore, but keep everything you do from now on the right level'

I was so amazed it felt like I heard the same words from the Lord when he spoke to the women In John verse 7:53-8:14, everyone accused her of adultery and the Lord let her accusers know "if anyone is without sin cast the first stone." No one could, so Jesus told her he would not condemn her and go sin no more.

It is so amazing when you see the word of God come alive in your face, at that time it was time for me to realize that I had a special calling on my life, and I could not accept anything or anyone to take me off track, I could not let my guard down at anytime. My Father in heaven deserves that much and more from us. This is another way I knew that still the Lord loves me and would never let us fall if our minds & heart is ready to do right, but never get it twisted you will go through, yes you would need to face some things you have done in your past, yes it is tough, but long as you got Jesus on the inside outside and around you, and you are ready to live that life on the straight and narrow road, he will hold and sometimes carry you through, yes history can repeat itself if you are dipping in the same past,

But God wants to wash it all away and cast it in the sea of forgetfulness, so stop the enemy from throwing it back up in your face by choosing the Lord today make Jesus Christ your Savior! And tell about all his goodness today.

We serve a forgiving God that does not want any of his children to fall and be cast aside, If only we would truthfully testify of how we have messed up and stop putting all the blame on the devil, some fault we are responsible for ourselves, do not forget about the choices God has given us, right or wrong, good or evil, I hear these words all the time amongst the people of God, Oh' the devil made me do it, or the devil had my mind messed up, Oh' the devil gave man or woman to me, Oh' the devil made me loose, the devil this, the devil that. The Devil cannot make us do anything that we don't want to do.

It is the lack of knowledge that makes us fall into diver's temptations, this is why we fall from the wayside, but if we keep our minds entirely on the Lord and what he has for us on how he wants us to live and walk,

By renewing our minds daily, staying in the word, praying without ceasing, then and only then will we be able to stand against the wiles of the enemy, the Power of God will allow us the right to rise through the angry tears and turn them into tears of Joy!

I have hurt and let down a lot of people God sent my way to minister to by allowing my emotions and feelings to determine the best of me, Instead of doing what God has for me to do and then learning how to step aside, let God finish what he has started. A lot of us mess up and let down people that we lead to Christ by allowing them to meet us, instead of God in us. We need to let them know no matter what title is in front of your name we are no better than them, and we are will make mistakes.

So believe the God in you, instead of the "I am" equal to God.

Let them know that you also need someone to minister to you as well, and that you get weary at times, and that you experience some of the same things in your walk with God, let them know the true testimony that lies behind that title and that you have been through what they are trying to come out of.

If we think about it and study our word we will see that God does not lead the dark into darkness, only the dark into light.

We cannot minister to someone concerning a problem that they are going through unless we have been through that test, and God has delivered us from it?

Remember every person that comes to you for your help to solve a problem does not mean you are the problem solver at that appointed time, this does not mean that you have not been called to teach, minister or counsel, but it just means that you do not have all the answers, but you do know someone who does.

"Jesus" God wants us to step aside and pass it on to someone else. Stop being selfish because this is a soul you are dealing with, you got to be very careful and prayed up to lead someone in the right direction without holding them for your own glory, Check this out' as two trains trying to use the same track without lights and no warning, sooner or later they will collide, this is just like souls trying to walk in the same direction, and both are weak trying to guide each other to their destination, One will pull the other because there is no strength to move forward, The Lord states this in his word, Mathew chapter 15 verse14,

They are blind leaders of the blind, if the blind lead the blind both shall fall into a ditch. "We haven't to be careful when we know that we are not where we should be in the Lord, and when we are going through a tribulation struggling within, and we feel ourselves falling, because we can cause someone else to fall, believe me, we have all been there' at one point of time in our lives we will be.

I know because I was myself feeling that I was untouchable, that the enemy was not going to test me again, or my Faith was not going to be tested. Some things are not only from Satan.

Some trails & tribulations come to test us for growth, the higher the calling, the higher the steps and the higher the enemy needs to send someone that can reach us, But know that he had to get permission first, there is nothing he can do to you in his own power, he has no power. Stop giving him praise, God through the hard times, stand through the longsuffering, you will & can make it!

Only gives his children power to resist so stand

I am making it!

I refuse to allow the enemy to defeat me, because I know that all power is in God's hand, it will not be easy, the road will become smoother, as long as you allow God to direct your path.

As my journey went on I knew I was forgiven from God, I still was not forgiven by my accusers, the ones that wanted me to fall, the ones who only sought to harm, the ones that were betting on my death. Here, we go with all the stones that had tried to expose her, shame her, persecute her, and kill her. Anyone the devil could mislead, or win over too attack me, the ones I love, ones that were dear to my heart, the ones that believed in me, the ones that I helped, the ones I fed, the ones God sent my way, funny but true, tell yourself if a stranger said bad things concerning you, would you care? Not really, because they really don't know you and you don't know them enough to care, What about the ones dear to your heart? The ones you know people would believe because these are the people that know you so well, so why would they lie on you? These are the ones Satan will use, the people that effect you so where it hurts, so when it comes full circle it is easy to open a cut deeper when it is already a wound that was not healed correctly,

I call it excisable revenge it could not get any sweeter.

This is why it is important to ask not only God for forgiveness, but also the ones you mislead, hurt or shown the wrong message from God, don't set your mind on worrying about if they have forgiven you, but concentrate on doing what is required of you, In James chapter 5 verses, 12-16 tells us to confess our faults one to another, pray for one another and we shall be forgiven of our sins, If they don't forgive, don't allow it to effect you, if God has forgiven you, than what can anyone else hold against you? Let it be well with you spirit and soul that it is finished, move forward and pray for them.

Leave with some the word of God, sometimes we need to be patient with one another they might not want to forgive you at that appointed time so keep them In prayer as someone had to pray for you, we cannot expect everyone to be in the same place that you are in.

Words Of Forgiveness!

Words for forgiveness: Mathew chapter 18 verse 21&22, Mathew 6: 14&15, Ephesians 4:32, Mark 11:25, Colossians 3:13, Luke 17:3&4, first John 1:9, Luke 6:37, Mathew 18-15. These are some of the places that teach me of forgiveness, words to live by, we as children of God have to realize that when we fall we had a chain of others falling with us, the ones that look at the light we shine, when it goes out the darkness comes again. So have compassion as Jesus did, pray with patients and do not judge the circumstances.

If the table were turned' how would you deal with it? You would not know until it had happened to you.

Even though, my heart still felt bad for what I did, I knew I had to move forward, I could not change the past, I was forgiven, God has given me another chance to prove my love to him, what an awesome God we serve! I had so many excuses of why I did what I had done, but all in all it still was sin, If I truly were a part of the body of Christ,

I had to depart from the things of the world, know that there are only certain types of power that the Lord gives us, and it is not the power of control how, and when we change someone's problems, that is only up to God,

He has the power to change all our storms, but he will give us the power to stand through it all no matter what. God is the all in all, he is the I am, the Problem solver, the Provider, the Healer, the Way maker. If only we truly take a stand and be honest with ourselves first, there is no perfect Christians, put the lord can give you something we all could use, Perfect Peace' if only we keep our mind stayed on him, and we wonder why he is worthy to be praised, as I study my word daily, I wake up and ask God to help me please, I got to read something from him daily that would put me and keep me on the right track, I don't always wake up and run straight to my word the bible, some days I get side tracked, and I find myself off focus,

So now lately I have been praying more asking the Lord to help me resist anything that is not like him, Resist anything that could keep me up set, depress, walking on the wrong path, give me the strength to seek him first, so all other things could be added. It is so easy for us to form, and open our mouths and tell others what they should do,

When we are really taking short cuts ourselves not being honest with ourselves that we are weak in our walk, and need some guidance ourselves, it is okay to come up short just ask God to fill what is missing.

Examining thyself, and do a reality check so you can become all you need to be in the Lord. All you need to do is ask and you shall receive. Knock and the door shall be opened.

The true lesson that I have learned would be, being honest no matter how bad the situation looks, know that God will turn a bad situation into a good one for his glory, he will give you a new perspective in your work with him,

God's light and way do not keep us blind to his ways, we can be blinded to God's light by not seeing the real truth of his blessings, What makes us hopeless and have a bitter attitude creeps right into our hearts when we are not equip with the full armor, some things we got to leave in God's hand, some people will only believe nothing but bad about another, someone who has fallen short on their walk with God refuse to hear anything good no matter how they have turned their lives around, or have apologized for their actions,

They would watch your life harder than their own, they will try to build more cases against if they could, They would twist all of your good into bad for no reason, but you still stay focus, God is the only one who can change the hearts of prejudice, gossip, jealousy, harden hearts, stiff neck spirits of an unforgiving heart, you just got to keep it moving, shake the mess off you and keep stepping, don't allow this to defeat you this too shall pass.

Do not allow any situation to become delectating to you that it would pull you from God. Only man counts your mistakes, God only counts how much you have grown, and how your attitude changes in the mist of it all, The test of your growth is the power of your stand with the knowledge you receive you will not receive a grade for your test, because you will keep on being tested until we get it right, and that is on judgment day! Our breakthrough will determine our growth and will reveal our knowledge and understanding of Gods greatest work in our life.

God will bless our later days just as he did Job. "Job 42:12" states as long as we remain faithful through our long suffering. God wants us to develop an unflinching faith through it all, James1: 2&3 we got to decide through it all if we want to move forward and live a successful life with God by stepping out of our past and moving forward into our present, when you have been forgiven from God, it should not matter how others remember your fall,

Know that it could not of been hard enough to have kept you down, the love of God have allowed you to made it to this point and whatever could have destroyed you is helping making you complete and free.

We have to get to a point where we surrender our entire past to the Lord. Walk By stepping out, come out of it' do not look back. 1Corinthians chapter 2 verse 9 states, that no eye or ear have heard or seen the heart of what God has prepared for those who love him.

So keep on walking my brothers and sisters and let's see what the end is going to be.

Stop worrying about your future, know God has it completely in his hand if we would just keep it with him, timing is everything I have been through and still experiencing, but it all works in our favor.

I am still on the hand clock of God's time he still works out all my problems and fixes the broken pieces, and molds my mind, my heart and unperfected peace. Something's that happen in our lives come with a warning, and some come without warning. Such as, when your heart is telling you not to go down a certain street, and you do anyway, and then something bad happens, or like when your heart tells you not to buy a new car or something that you just had to have and you do, but then drastically you lose your job, and the means to pay on what you new you could not afford it. Another scenario could be that when you do something bad, thinking you are helping someone, but in your heart you know it is wrong you do it anyway. Even if your heart lets you know it isn't right. You then find yourself in a messed up situation that could have had you imprisoned or worse, the only person that could get you out of it would be God,

These things are what we considered without warning, sudden death of a loved one, accidents, and natural disasters, God always sends his people warnings when we are falling short from his glory, when we are making a left instead of a right,

When we start losing our way, God gives us warnings before destruction. Proverbs 1-32, Psalms 60-4, Deuteronomy chapter 8 vs. 19-20 read so really

That we have no excuse, please tell me why we use so many? Flesh is the thing that separates us from God and keeps us from being what we need to be.

This is why the flesh should die daily, because if we don't control it, it surly would control us straight to hell! We cannot control it with our own knowledge or wisdom, it can only be controlled by God knowledge and his word, which gives us instructions on what and how we need to handle it, We need to have a schedule for everyday that tells us our training days with the word, being affective for God takes training that only God can teach us,

It is a lot to get equipped for your salvation, even, though it is free, we still need to know what is required for the strength to stand through the angry tears.

In some part of our walk we have to develop the power to stand when God starts to expose some of our mess, so that we can see our filthy self before it destroys us, this is what had to happen for me to get totally right because I had an awesome call on my life and every fifty thing that would hinder me for the assignment I was chosen for, he had to separate me from the hurt, pain & shame so that I could be purge from the circle that was heading me straight for destruction, It was time for Self-evaluation,

I had to see my own full-length mirror of sin I had painted all by myself, it was time to stop blaming everything on Satan, the step that we all need to see is, 1. I had to see the disobedience spirit in you, 2. See that lack of spiritual knowledge in me, 3.

See the self righteous spirit in you, 4. See that I can allow myself to do all this, by myself and no one forced me, 5. See that denial spirit and when you get exposed from the junk you have put into your journey, don't get upset, get happy that God had called you into the marvelous light, thank him for allowing you to be free realizing that I was destroying myself by believing that I was doing something for self gain rather it was helping or not, it was wrong the way it was done, and I knew this, now that was the sin of it. This is why I love the lord the way I do, and you should too, I know he has done the same for you, and if you say no I never sinned then you just did, it does not matter what you did sin is sin, big or small God despise it all so this is why he has called us out of darkness, The Lord did not allow this to destroy our destiny that is connected to him, praise him right now not later, and give him the praise that is due to him, God has not turned his back or his hand, God has shown his mercy, and his grace, God had to show me that I was chosen and not just called, What about you?

What have you done lately that you have been hiding and scared to let anyone know you got yourself in, a mess that you can't see your way out, what have you allowed yourself to be a prisoner for? Well I am here to tell you just give it to the Lord, let me tell you a little secret' he already knows about it so what are you waiting on? Cast it to him, and watch him work it out for his Glory.

A lot of us suffer with mental habits and we run from doctor to doctor, trying to get our minds healed, and the only thing we receive is a pill for this, a pill for that. All that does is prolong the mental statistics the issues are still there, the only doctor that can heal that mind is Doctor Jesus, by renewing our minds daily in the word of God and restore the right spirit within us, when this change starts then we would feel and see a difference, are habits start changing, from bad to good.

Our walk, talk, praise, prayers and social life will have a different outlook, The more we get experience with God the easier you can find peace with all the decisions you make even when you have made a mistake, we cannot predict the future, only God know what lies ahead, he knows what we will do before we do it, Just stay in his will and keep reaching toward his direction, the reason we are so **unstable** is that we give so many people our responsibilities for our personal joy, If our happiness depended on others than we would truly never be happy, until we learned to do things God way we will always be in chaos and keep going in circles,

Our life's will not be reaching for its true purpose without God there is no plan, nor a purpose for that plan, how can we expect to see changes within our own lives, if we are constantly talking to others about our problems, instead of how God can and will s fixed the problems before it has happened?

Give God the praise in advance and be of good courage, darkness can only lead you toward light when you are searching for God, defeat can only arise you to victory, The only way we can reach that goal is constantly stay connected to God in true worship,

Speak your change and watch it come to past, Psalms chapter 44 verses 7&8; this is what I am doing daily, thanking God for all his Grace & Mercy of how he has lifted my shame, how he has given me another chance, God is so good, and this is why I praise him, I have learned a great lesson out of thinking that because I was one of God children I could get away without answering for my sins, This is when God had exposed me more, Think about it, why would he need to expose you while you are already still in sin?

People already know what you are doing, What about us, the ones that hide behind the title, yes you teacher, preacher, pastor, evangelist, choir leader, ministers, young leaders deacon, missionaries, mothers and all those that say they are saved and living a righteous life, let it be known that you are not perfect and it is a battle between the flesh & spirit, and if we all want to walk through the garden then know that your radar will go off if you are hiding it, God will expose those that he has chosen, It is not to harm you or tear you down, but to build you and lift you to your next level, We must give up the lower life to obtain the higher life in God, Mathew chapter 10 verse 39 say; we must decide not desire the things of the world and desire the things in heaven.

It is time to choice the greater, heaven and leave the earth behind, Psalms chapter 73 verse 25, So throw off everything that is hindering you, that thing called sin the thing so easy to entangle with, and let us run together with perseverance toward the race marked out for us.

Hebrews 12: we can only gain this as we deny fleshly desires and ourselves, we owe this much because we do not belong to ourselves but to the one who has made us free "Jesus". Anything that worries us, rather than keep us spiritual or temporal, anything that keeps us from fellowship, is to be put away and kept away literally!

In Romans chapter 6, verse 23, It give you insight on having freedom in God, become new in the spirit renewal of the mind and put on the new self, become more like God, righteous and holy in his troth, Ephesians chapter 4 verses 22-24: You could never have too much self-examination, believe me, too little can head you in a messed up situation, "Been there done that!

"Knowing the difference"

I have learned now to move forward, as I look back over my flaws and shortcomings as a Christian I have realized Satan can do absolutely nothing to mess up the love Christ has for me, but I can separate myself from feeling it the love, but no one can take it.

I laugh as I say, "How could I ever believe that the devil lies, his insidious lies, Accusing God and others. HA, HA I am on too you now Devil!" the worst burden or problem I ever had to carry in my life so far was, myself. Now that could be hard to deal with knowing, that having to manage self, is laying and taking all burdens' your whole-self in God hands to care for by trusting he knows what's best for us. When I found my true identity in Christ, I could see my wholeness being made' the only thing God want from us is our hearts, and just believe and have faith in him for everything, If I would of done just that I would of not been in the some of the situations I put myself in, just look how God loves us, I know he loves me because I did not deserve his grace and mercy.

After all the one thing I needed to do was stay close to him when things were going wrong, Run to the Lord even when it get to hard to bear, run as fast as you can, because the devil is on your tracks, so don't turn back.

I should He was on my tracks so hard, he could have stopped me from writing this for you to hear my testimony. I could have been doing 5 to10 yrs in prison because of my lack of knowledge, and it was not because God did not equip me with it, I just got lazy and comfortable in my walk with God I started taking breaks instead of depending on God, But God! I could have been divorce today, not because God said, but because I was not patient long enough to wait on God's change, I tried to change everything myself.

I have been praying more when the devil was attacking, instead of fighting back, But God!

I could have been running from place to place, state to state because things was not going the way I wanted them to go or seeing a progress in my faithfulness, I was not patient enough to be still and see God bring it to past, But God!

I could of gave up on writing my second book because I was filling the vision or word I received from God has not came to past yet, But God! I thank God for allowing me to spend this time with him, writing every thought down and searching through his word and hearing him tell me what to write and sharing my testimony, having an great intimacy with God, I love it.

I think that it is great to write down everything you go through and praise him for it all. Keeping notes then going back to read them over and over again, keeps you moving and jumping for the Lord.

Seeing and watching how he saves you from yourself as well as keeping you from the enemies hands time after time, after time, Just think of how many times God has rescued you from yourself,

When you knew you were doing wrong, just to see if you could get away with it, Or get yourself caught up and did not know how to get free from it, Here comes God, just around the corner saying: "baby girl or baby boy, I have forgiven you, go in peace and sin no more,

Now why do we still feel like we need to get approval from others to move on and let go of our past?

When God has already forgiven you? If we keep trying to please man, than we will not and cannot be a servant for God. Galatians chapter 1 verse 10; This could be a great burden trying to see if and when people are pleased by our performance, this way of thinking has to be thrown away. This is what we call (People Pleaser) this will only lead you to bondage within. John chapter 12 verses 42 and 43 gives us an example of peer pressure, we think our youth today are the only ones that deal with this on a day to day basis,

But no, we as Christians have the same kind of pressure thrown at us from work, friends, and family.

This is Sometimes it simply comes from holding a certain title, a piece of paper is not what you need to get into heaven, So, when you fall, get it right with God, don't worry about what others say keep on running your race, Trust I know this is where I found myself trying to keep people pleased with me, But not to speak of my pain, my hurt, my failures, my faults, my depression, my shortcomings, my mistakes,

I did not want anyone to look down on me. So, I pretended that I was not human, something we do when we worry about what others think or say about us. Forget that, it is a daily process this Christian walk, and we will have a past that we can call a testimony in our present life, and it is a wonderful, joyful thing to have. Without a past, how could we expect to have a future?

Why it is in the word of God that we can overcome anything by one another testimonies, because out of the heart flows the issues of life, As we read our word daily and fellowship by going to a bible teaching, a place of God, one that believes that Jesus is God only begotten son and that he gave himself ransom for our sins, died so that we may have life and have it to the fullness, When I realized it was me that needed to pick up my cross and follow it where my destiny was headed, I had to leave something's behind, these things could not follow me where I was going, when I tried to bring them, the road got harder and longer, we can slow up our own process,

We can blame Satan all we want but God has equipped us to drive ahead, he made the road easy for us to follow and made our burden lighter, but we will tend to make it difficult and heavy by our own disobedience to what our Lord tells us.

Press Your Way!

God knows what is best for us at all times, Mathew chapter 19 verse 30; "let us know that if we leave everything and everyone for the love of God and his name sake, "Jesus" and pick up our cross we will inherit eternal life" believe me Satan will try his best to use his 12 disciples' called "hindrance" to keep you off focus, but will you leave it all behind for Jesus sake? Your: 1.House, 2. Jobs, 3.Mother, 4.Father, 5.Sisters, 6.Brothers, 7. Children, 8.Husband, 9.Wife, 10.Friends or Enemies, 11.Fame, 12.Self.

These are the things that could be in the heart, things that will flow out your inheritance to the Kingdom of God. The devil knows what and when to use these 12 disciples to stop or prolonged your destiny, but the question is will you forsake all when the time comes for you to move forward?

We just can't get ourselves caught up in anything that will take away the love we have for the Lord, He is a jealous God, if we put these things before him as if they were more important than God, then we are headed for destruction, I can remember a time when I choose some of these things before my relationship with God and I had to fall and believe me some of the falls were pretty hard to handle, if it had not been for the Merciful God we serve who has forgave me and did not give up on me, My mind is made up now, so I could not tell you where I would have been, but I do know for sure writing this book for you, helped me release, relate, and relax so whatever you are doing and whatever you are making more important than God, Stop it! Stop it now! Ask God for forgiveness, repent and move forward, start forming a serious personal relationship with the one that truly matters the most in all our lives, Jesus,

Then watch your life unfold some awesome things you have been waiting and longing for to happen in your life. God blesses and cares that his children inherits the promise he gave to all mankind, everlasting life with him.

It is up to us if you want it bad enough, The three things the Lord, has given to us, this is talked about in Corinthian chapter 13 verses 14: 1.Faith, 2.Hope, 3.Love and with all these things the greatest one is "love" This is amazing!

Thinking back, I read in his word that the first shall be last and last will be first. The Lord gave us love when he died for all our sins, so that we might have faith to believe him and his word. Faith is the first thing that we need to have for this all to work, if we have hope, if we believe his love, the kind-of that has no limits, If you walk with him and look to him for your every need, expect help from him he will never fail you In Psalms chapter 84, verse 11: tells us that there is no good thing that the Lord would with hold from those who walk upright and good.

So do not be of foolish things, but be doers of good things of God, some good things could be peace of conscience, joy in the Holy Spirit, in our life and when he returns we will have fruition of God's presence, the vision of his blessed face.

These are some good things God has bestowed upon us (his children).

> We just got to trust God for his word, trust does not
> come over night, it comes with a relationship, with
> our walk and it requires commitment, Know that God
> is trusted worthy, confident; this is why he seeks our
> good, believe me he still loves me, inspire of all my
> flaws, Now think about it, take your time and think
> to yourself how much love would someone give to you
> if they knew you were messed up from the floor up.

> I know of one, God' he loves us in-spite of and
> show this love every day. When we develop a close
> relationship with God, comes and intimacy, yes,
> intimacy' one that is unlike any other touch or feeling.

When you enter into a natural relationship with someone you like what he or she does, you want to give him or her all the respect. So what would make God different, the one who created us? The fact is, God wants and needs our respect in the relationship he develops with us you cannot have true and great intimacy without respect. In Psalms chapter 96; the psalmist speaks a lot about God's very nature and what he commands from us,

> Reverence, respect, our fear, and to let others know of
> the love and relationship we have with him. We need to
> show that we live totally for him and we don't want to
> disappoint our true walk with him, no matter what else
> looks or sounds good, We have to show honor to him at
> all cost, make a stand that we belong to him and serve
> him and no other Gods, In Psalms chapter 25 verses
> 4&5 it is a deep saying; it reads about letting God know

that you are totally sold out for and to him, that you depend on him for everything! Show me your ways,

O' Lord teach me your path, lead me in your truth, teach me, for you are the God of my salvation. Now this is what I love to read and say, to remind myself that God is in charge and I need his guidance everyday' Here I am in another season, the enemy is getting weary and another attack has come on me this time it hit harder than ever before. A separation in my heart, an attack on my children to come up against me, I got to stop writing for a minute and laugh if I don't I will cry, my joy is my strength, I need it right about now!

Well, what can I say, but to tell you the truth I am mad, I am angry, I am ready for a serious battle, My children and grandchildren our very, very, very deep, in my heart, the enemy knows this, man he Is off the hook, Lord, Lord, Lord is all I can say. Savoir, Savoir, Savoir, is all I can depend on, the Blood, the Blood, and The Blood is my anchor hold, my shield, my covering. Hallelujah! Hallelujah! Halleluiah! This is my call for power, I know this is not about me, I know why this is happening, I am not afraid because I am walking through the shadow of death,

God is with me and he will comfort me and in the right season it will be alright. Because this too shall pass away, but God word will stand concerning my life. Lord, here I am again wondering what I have done wrong my babies mind, I know I have not done it all right, I know what had to be expose for me to move forward but, Lord my babies don't allow the enemy to have my babies protect them Lord, guard my heart on what is happening, I know this dart is going to hurt more than ever before, so as I go through the forest fire, Lord hold my hand and keep reminding me that I am your chosen vessel, So I can keep a smile and shine all the way through.

I truly thought that coming clean, coming out of the closet, telling my life story was going to bring my babies and I closer than ever before. But I forgot to tell them the truth of one lie that can destroy I was not PREPARED FOR ALL THIS! I was hurt when my family turned their back on me, not reaching out to get to know me and release all their hidden scars, so that they can heal.

One thing I never knew would be that my babies would pull so far away, the devil is a liar, you will not take over my foundation, he has laid this foundation for me to stand and I will not be moved until the Lord say so, if we got to lose everything and everyone to be closer to Jesus than strip me Lord and re-clothe me with what you have for me Jesus. My relationship with my sons was soar my relationship with my daughter grew cold. I mean it was eating me in places I can't explain. The more it attacked me, the more I fast and prayed and called out to the Lord, I said please help me, I feel like I am falling like I never felled before, maybe because I never knew that a lie could separate me and my kids due to us only having each other,

Please catch me. My relationship was not right with my son we had messed up separation, then I lose my relationship and bond with another son, to top it off my first Born, my daughter, my twin, my praise, my stronghold, my best friend.

I know Lord that you say not to love anything or anyone more than you, but I felt like I did.

My heart would not pump like it use to, I was having chest pains every night, for two months non-stop, I felt like I was fading away, I wanted to live so that I could see what the end was going to be. I did not want to give up, I knew I was over it, but it had felt like the clock was moving and I was stuck on my past. Every time I looked around, it felt as though other Christians were being blessed, everything in their favor I looked up to the sky and said, Lord, my daddy, my father, who is the creator of all situations, would you look down on me and rain, power on me to keep me running, because my walk has slowed down.

I need some soles that are made of cotton so that
I could not feel the heaviness that is weighing me
down, my mind is made up, I will not give up, I know
that God loves me no matter what it looked like,

This is not my revelation, I know what was spoken in my life concerning me, I shall live and not die, I, shall run and not faint, my tears had been wiped by the power of God hands, He has given me power to stand through any storm. This too shall pass, when it do we will come together and it will be stronger than before, what a day that will be, So I will wait and continue to praise you Lord, I will praise my way through! I can say one thing, it has only been a little while but God has been working good things over my husband, our bond, our relationship has grown stronger, we are reading and praying, discussing what God has been doing with us, Thank you Jesus! My husband has been encouraging me through it all, No it is not perfect, what marriage is? Though I am seeing a mighty change I would of walked away then I would have not received my blessing of what God was and is doing,

A husband that loves the Lord, seeking how to be more and more like him, a man that is after Gods own heart, I have a husband that care and loves me, He will give himself to be what he needs to be and not give up trying,

No matter how much he may fall, but the important thing he gets back up and asks God to help him be a better husband for me, thank you Lord! What I am facing and feeling now, I don't know what I would have done if he was not here to hold me up and push me to not give up, We are going to fight until the end! My birthday is tomorrow, September 1, I am blessed to see another day, Just knowing that I can wake up and have another day to spread the goodness of Jesus and all he has done for me, Writing my second book is more than enough to shout about, I am thanking God that I trust him in the tough times as we grow closer to God the devil never stops poking at your flesh,

He knows that he is really defeated and hates to be exposed to Gods children.

He wants you to think he is powerful, he wants you to believe that he has reign over your life, he wants you to believe that you will never make it through your trail's and tribulations, he wants you to give up and give in to all his lies and tricks, I realize that the enemy will never leave me alone, he knows the closer I get to my destiny, he needs to try to pull me back or grab onto the strings, he dreads that he can't grasp onto me, the more that I hangs around trying to seek and devour, the more I run toward the Lord.

We got to stop getting to comfortable in our walk with God, no time to seat until they day he tell you well done my good and faithful servant, what I mean is when we sit around, relax, the enemy attacks get stronger, always keep a head start never allow Satan to catch up with you, always stay ahead then he will not be able to trick your mind into thinking that he is equal to you, he will try to defeat you okay, you just got to overcome the hurdles, but know that there will be more higher jumps to be made,

So keep up the pace in God he has your back so don't look back to see who is behind you, always stay focus on the one who matters, Always look ahead of you because that is the one who truly holds life and death of your race. I have to tell you that it is not easy being a child of God, but it is rewarding and I love seeing the achievements that I have and will receive along the way, the path that I follow keeps me lifted and fulfilled all the way, I never get tiered or faint, or discouraged like I used to,

I just get excited to see what the end is going to be, so why should we give up? Before we know what our end result will be. My cross may feel heavier as time fades, but I feel my feelings getting lighter and I am able to walk as long as I keep focused, on what is ahead of me and never looking backward. Every word God has spoken to and about me will not come back void! How will we ever know that if we give up before we finish the race? His word tells us that what he has started in us, he will finish it till the end, How will we know if we give up now? I don't know about you, but I want to know what my end is going to be, so I will push my way through the crowd of jealousy, backbiters, false accusers, haters, false prophets so that I could get to the real deal, Every time I take a moment to think about what I went through on yesterday, I scream "Glory"

Every time I make it through another morning and
I arise, to see the sun shining and the birds sing
outside my window I shout "Glory" every time
I can stand and feel my toes, and feel my arms,
and I can walk and talk I scream "Glory"!

Every time I can remember my name and who my husband
and children are I scream "Glory" every time I can pick up
a bible and read a word from God, and get excited I scream
"Glory" God has kept his hand on me and has not allowed
me to be lost, I have to just stop where I am and give God
all the praise and sing I got a feeling everything is going to
be all right, be all right, everything is going to be all right.

Then another praise song will follow,

No Break The Cycle!

Can't no body do me like Jesus, can't no body do me like the Lord, can't no body do me like Jesus, because he is my friend. We might go through hardship and it will feel overwhelming, but when it is said and done look at the big picture and see that the Lord has and will never forsake you. I know that I am love by the all mighty, the creator of heaven and earth, the one, who is the beginning and the end. So why should I be afraid of any obstacle?

Why should I be afraid? You can just pick up your bible turn to psalms chapter 23 vs. 4-6; "yea though I walk through the shadow of death, I will fear no evil, for thou art with me, thy rod and thy staff comfort me. Thou prepares table before me in the presence of my enemies; thou anoints my head with oil, my cup runeth over, surely goodness and mercy should follow me all the days of my life. And I will dwell in the house of the Lord forever, we got to realize and believe that Jesus is the son, the begotten Son of God, and if he sent his only begotten son to die for us, than why would we doubt his power?

Why do we doubt that we can't make it? It is time for us to wake up from the day dreaming state that we are in, and know that the battle is not ours it is the Lords.

The battles we are trying to fight have already been won by God, and receive the strength from the Lord. To stand through the tears, we got the power through the blood of Jesus! Psalms chapter 27th and vs. 4 states, "let us know that the Lord is our light and salvation; he is our strength of living. Know who should be afraid of.

We have to know that when the enemy comes up against us, to pick and eat at our flesh, we will stumble, we will fall, as long as we continue to seek after the Lord; he will hide us in his pavilion. The secret place of his tabernacle and place us on a rock that is so solid to stand on and higher than our enemies could ever reach. I just got it reminded to me of this song that Michael Jackson song, you know "I'm Bad" I'm bad the devil knows it.

And there is nothing he can do about it! So why do we find ourselves giving in every time the devil barks? He is like a dog that barks, but can't bite; he has no teeth, Ha, ha, ha! All he does is nibble on the flesh, and it feels numb. When we are in the right place with God, the only way you should feel his bite through the flesh is when we are slipping, sliding, in your walk with God. Get back or get in you rightful place with the Lord. So, know that you can receive the power to stand through the fight & the angry tears I have to admit I have fallen plenty of times, and I have had to call on help to get back up,

And get back in my rightful place, a place I needed to be to receive the Power to make a firm stand on the foundation God has for me to stand on.

As I have been writing this book, I have had so many spirits to deal with, these spirits did not want

me to write this or to share that we are more than
conquers, But the enemy did not and do not want
to let us go no matter what price was given,

He knows that he has been defeated and that the battle
was already won, you tell me who knows a cheerful loser?
The devil has been exposed, when Jesus died on Calvary
and he knows that his time is now to lose all of Gods
children. So, he tries to win as many as he can to keep by
his side, he will do all that he can, to keep you from the
destination point, By lying, stealing, killing, destroying,
hurting, blaming, you for his lost. This is why we are
attacked daily. Our flesh does not want to surrender to sin,
It hates to die, it loves living and it needs a body to reside
in and a spirit to feed on, so that it can gain power to live!"

I talked about how to open up hidden wounds that were
still infected and that needed to be cleansed and healed
from Gods children. It showed you how to be set free, but
infection does not want to leave, no matter what exposure
it had. By spreading the seed I bared the ones I loved and
the enemy that did not want me to become clean, but the
devil is a liar. I have heard my calling and was set free.

I was made whole to step out on faith and believe
that I was going to make it no matter what came
my way. I knew then I was given the power to resist
anything that was not like God and the power to stand
through any test. There was nothing that the enemy
could do to me without the permission from God.

So why should I fret?

Some of us are still in the first grade, if it was given
permission to attack, then God has given me the
right shield and cover to stand through it.

But I have to be in the right place to receive, what is our
excuse? We cannot and will not find one that will explain
why we get taken under, when God himself has given us the
answer already, If only we would seek, there is a show that
comes on TV, which asks you, smarter than a fifth grader?

How can we be if we are still in the first grade?

Because we started reading at the beginning, but we had
stopped and rushed to the end to fast, without stopping
to read the most important part the middle, the part
that had all the ingredients we needed, the answers
that would of slowed us down, wait on the Lord, who
renewals our strength, to carry us through the wiles of
the enemy, but we were too much in a hurry to finish and
wanted to completed. How did we gain the knowledge
and wisdom of a fifth grader? We did not study at all,
if we did then we would of came across the scripture
in Isaiah chapter 40 verse 31, they that wait upon the
Lord shall renew their strength they should mount up
with wings of eagles. They should run and not be weary,
they shall walk, not faint, and before he told us that,
he said in verse 29, he gives power to the faint and to
them that have no might, he increases strength, So what
excuses do we have? That we can't go on or we just give
up, or feel like the enemy has won the battle, so let's ask
ourselves again, "are we smarter than an a fifth grader?

What grade truly are we in? I ask myself that every time I
feel that I can't go on, this is when I call on Jesus, to help

me to the next level, remember, Jesus was twelve years old, when his mission began, If you are on milk, with the word, then stay there until God evaluates you, and moves you to another level, don't allow yourself to jump to the meat of the word if you have not digested the milk fully yet. Whole milk, 2%, or 1% milk, will not do. It is watered down. I rather drink the right milk for years before, someone gives me meat and has me to choke on it for not being able to swallow and digest it before my time. This is how the enemy, will have our minds think, but if the mind is not being renewed, then who is thinking for you? The word of God tells us not to be anxious to do or go ahead of the Lords plan for our lives, he will exalt you in due time.

So many Christians feel that they are hearing from God about their life, running out for others to pray for them, or to get a prophecy about who and what they are in Christ remember he is a regular man, people laying hands on one another and giving a prophecy like it is just some words to be thrown around but when our prayers are not seeming like they are answered or the prophesy' don't come to light, we start doubting God.

The word tells us; suddenly not to lay hands on anyone and it tells us also in Mark chapter 13 vs. 21thru 23: Then if any man shall say to you there is Christ, believe him not for false Christ's and false prophet, shall rise and shall show signs and would seduce, even the very elect will be fooled if we don't listen to the warnings God is given us in his word.

It is important to study your word, read, fast, and pray always without ceasing so that you will not fall into the enemy traps. I have been fooled so many times, due to my lack of knowledge, and wanting to

run before I walk, listening to God word through
others concerning my call and not directing it
back to God so that he can have the last say.

We can easily get caught up with the excitement f
just wanting to be changed, noticed, and accepted,
we just go with the flow of what sounds good. So,
beware, stay where God can reach you by staying
in your word, communicate always with God, just
picture this in your mind, Some would say that it is
hard to talk to God, because we cannot see him.

Think about it the next time you tell a complete stranger
you just met your business' it was easy to talk to them. Or
another thought, when you go on an interview, you really
don't know what to expect, but you go on the interview
trusting that you may have the job. This is the same
when talking to the Lord, the only difference is when you
present a resume to God, and you receive a good report.

You find yourself blessed, and when you talk to God you get
results to know that he was listening, and will fix whatever
the problem is or was but with that stranger, he cannot fix
the problem and he or she might not of paid any attention to
what you were saying and on that job interview they heard
you when you said you really need this job because of bills or
family, but they told you they would get back to you but, and
never did, but when you told God that you needed your bills
paid or you needed to feed your family, God provided it right
on time, so more you put in the more he gives, a hesitation,
now how does it you feel knowing that you can put all your
trust in this person you cannot see but you can feel all the
benefits. Glory! What a shout! If it is like that favors the, more
you put in the more he gives to you. I sit day after day and

seeing how God provides for his people' and it just pleases my soul knowing he never closes his eyes or took a nap.

When I need him the most which is every day of my life, tell me, who can you find that will stay with you no matter what? I am writing my play to my first book, we will perform it in August of 20011 and man it has its ups and down, but if I don't take my off God he will not take his eyes off you me who will wipe my tears away? Had me so messed up with continued praise it was hard to write this book, but God. I am so excited working on this project, sometimes I cannot sleep just thinking about what god is bringing tomorrow I love that God is using me in ways I thought I would never be used in this way me a play writer, me an author, me a counselor, me an evangelist, me a mother, me a wife, me a sister, but if I take a letter out of each word it lets me know I am his servant, and I love it, I am sitting here tired and still listening to God he just spoke in my spirit that I will be writing another book Jesus is all I can say!

I tell you when you are working for the Lord you go to be prayed up, fast up because flesh will rise up in a heartbeat, I don't like t blame everything on the devil, u because we read our word we would know that he has no power to stand. If we don't give him legs, he has no arms he has no ears to hear if we don't speak it into existence, he has no voice to speak if we don't lend him our tongue he has no eyes to see if we don't keep it dark, so think about it all you got to do is resist him, and he will flee. You got the power when Jesus gave it up for you, use it wisely. Stop judging another because when it is all said and done we will be judged, I got to start on the next book Jesus said Thanks shout out to my Lord and savior, my love, the love of my life, my everything my reason to live, Jesus Christ.

My Heartfelt Thank you!

Thanks to my Husband, My children, my grandchildren, special thanks to, I would like to thank Sister Phyllis Evans & Brother Gabriel Suber for the song "Who Will Wipe My Tears Away?" Pastor Monica Phillips for the song "Who will wipe my Angry Tears? And my lovely niece Aquilla Hynes for the hit song "Who will Wipe My Tears Away? The Earlina Song

And special thanks to Joyce Myers, they are my Pillows when I need the cushion in holding on to the Gospel Play Who Will Wipe My Tears away?

I dedicate this book to a very special Auntie Willie Mae Ford, I love you for never Judging me, but believing in who I am, I love you both a

Strong Hold My Aunt Willie Bea, my Aunt Cleo Mosley!

Making a stand seems to be very difficult, but of you really truly on the Lord you would know that he is the one that stands for you. Even when the storm seems to be getting rough and you do not see any escape,

And you feel that the only option is to fall. The word tells us to stand, and do all that we can' after we have tried all that we can, so rest assure that God will do the rest.

We cannot allow our circumstances to overtake us. We have no power to fix or handle every day-to-day life problems. Or the power to help everyone we come in contact with. The reason why I am saying this is because; I can give you another testimony, which will explain the goodness and awesome God we serve. Make an example of making a stand through tears.

In today generation we need to open up more with our children and let them know of the tricks that the Enemy would try in their life, there is no new tricks under the sun that the enemy would bring, if it did not work with you believe me he would and will try it with the next generation, so let's break the chains' God gave us brains to open up the knowledge he is giving us in his word, and the revelation on how to resist all temptations, you got to let go of the old man so that God can put on the new man.

In I Colossians chapter 3 verses 9 &10 tells us to put off the old man with his deeds and put on the new man which is renewed in knowledge after the image of him that created us, Even when you are walking with the lord know that everything can look good for a while but don't be surprise that Satan is ramping and roaring waiting until he can attack again so be on guard with the whole armor of God,

Christ is looking for committed followers so that we can be good spiritual mentors and leaders.

If you want to know if my trials and tribulations stop! I would ask you, have Jesus returned yet?

All I can tell you is that I am dedicating my life daily to the lord, I am walking on that straight and narrow road, toward eternal life, I am trying to lay all my heavy burdens and trying to be submissive and obedient to God,

Know that my mind is made up and I will not turn back, I know that this battle is not mine it is and always belong to the lord, His word promise me that in Revelation chapter 21 verse 4 and God shall wipe away all Tears from our eyes, and there shall be no more death, neither sorrow, nor crying, neither shall there be any more pain: for the former things are passed away!!!

I want to thank and praise God for how he gave me strength through this whole book, to be able to release my story, my testimony' God has truly been my Anchor hold, he has took be back and through this like a soldier, and I hope and pray someone out there that reads this story realize that God is not a respect of person.

In Romans chapter 2 verse 11 has giving me another chance he has brought me out of darkness and into his marvelous light, truly through the mist of it all I have not always been faithful or true and have done a lot of damage and hurt one that I have love through my own self pity, I have not always trusted God to pull me through even when he had showed me his hand, and surly have not always obeyed him, but check this out" when the devil thought he had sink signed and delivered my feet on sinking sand God snatched me out just in time, for his purpose and plan' he is an on time God!

I am a living witness of the Devine, Agape love of God has for us,

Thank You Wonderful Counselor, Prince of Peace the Mighty God!

God has more stories out there, and he wants them to be told, he wants to help your growth in him, build your faith in him, and trust in him.

We overcome by one another testimony!!!

Now that the truth is out concerning by testimony, and my life,

Pray that I have reached someone to come clean come out that hidden closet and stop looking at the trick mirror the enemy set before us, and get it right before it is too late, I don't know how God would have you do it, it might not be In a book, but someway the lord will make it known to you, I know that my children will have a lot of question, but I know that the seed that God have in us will make us stronger to help another family, I did not write this story for compassion or pity, God has given me all that I need to overcome, what is coming ahead. All I and my family need is your prayers, because the enemy is mad that this had came out, I allowed him to have too much control over my family inherits, and now it is time to let God have full control and start driving us to our destiny,

Some things are in God timing so that it will heal the way it needs to be healed, so don't rush out and give all your goods to the dogs, wait on the lord make sure that it is God that is specking to you, I have tried to write this book for over 15 years and could not, I could relate in all areas of life and help minister to the souls of God children, I just thank God for his patience that he had on me, and all my ups and downs and turn a rounds, he never left me nor did he forsake me through the hot mess. It is so funny how we just do not realize that a family generational curse could follow you through many generations, and keep you in bondage, did you realize when it first happened in reading my story?

Well it happened first from my Mom, Then my grandmother home, then the child protection service, then the church, and last me, and if I did not realize the plot no matter how hard I tried to stop it from happening to my daughter it still happened, because I did not have God all the way!

So the trick of the enemy stops know, in this family tree from my next generation, and to give you another tip, when my mother past, my uncles came down for the funeral and I loved them just like God had first ordain for me to do, there was not pain or hurt that I felt toward them, I have totally forgiven them, I hug them and was not afraid, but happy and glad to see them, the past is behind us and I am moving forward to a awesome life with the lord.

Stay tune for the next awesome testimony of the next book God is starting in me. You just don't know how mad the devil is at me for letting go and letting God, so pray!

Love you All!!!

My daughters Poems

Who will wipe my tears away?

Who will carry each drop I pray

You reach a hand out and try to understand,

But you see each teardrop I've carried came from man

One who promised to keep me safe?

One who have said I was a disgrace,

Through the years I have learned to tuck my feelings inside,

Each teardrop is where my pain resides.

One by one they do fall

A story behind them all.

I have planned to keep them to myself,

On Gods secret mantel; tucked on a self.

Until I heard an angel say,

Young woman God will wipe each tear away,

From my eyes there shall be no more

The tears that lay lie behind a human door.

This angel replied no more sorrow, no more crying, no more dying.

There shall be no more pain for former things have passed away.

Because God and only God can wipe my tears away. Written by: My daughter Theresa Gilford

Faithful Seed

If you have and no one knows

Trust the lord and see it grow,

Seek for his truth, and his loving guidance

Follow his word, even if all you hear is silence

The lord may hide his face for maybe a month or two

But that doesn't mean that he is still not watching over you

Sad times may come and peaceful times may go

Yet that seed in your heart will still surely show

Stay on your knees, and pray to our father above

Let's give thanks to the lord for his unfailing love.

Written by my Step daughter Latisha Weaver

About Evangelist Earlina Gilford- Weaver

ABOUT ME!
WHO I WAS, AND WHO I AM NOW.

I WROTE THIS BOOK OF MY LIFE TO LET YOU KNOW THAT THIS REALLY HAPPENS IN LIFE STRUGGLES AND IN OUR DREAM FAMILIES TODAY, AND TO LET YOU KNOW THAT YOU CAN OVER COME, NO MATTER WHAT YOU HAVE AND GOING THROUGH IN YOUR LIFE YOU CAN FIND YOUR TRUE IDENTY THROUGH THE LORD, HE WILL AND CAN WIPE YOUR TEARS AWAY IF YOU WOULD JUST GIVE HIM ALL YOUR BURDENS, LAY IT AT HIS FETT AND JUST STEP ASIDE AND WATCH YOUR LIFE BLOOM.

WHO I WAS!

I WAS A LOST SOUL, DAMAGED GOODS, AND FEARFUL OF LIFE AND OTHERS, I HAD NO IDENITY OF WHO I WAS, AND WAS NUMBED THROUGH LIFE'S UPS AND DOWNS, I LIVED IN A LIFE THAT ONLY TOOK THE ROOLERCOASTER THAT TOOK ME UP AND DOWN AND THE MERRY GO ROUND THAT ONLY WENT IN CIRCLES

WHO I AM!

I AM A DEDICATED SERVANT OF THE LORD, A LOYAL WIFE AND A MOTHER OF THREE, A STEP MOTHER OF FIVE AND I HAVE FIVE GRANDCHILDREN, AND FIVE GOD CHILDREN, I AM A SPRITUAL MOTHER TO THE CHILDREN IN MY COMMUNITY, I AM A EVANGELIST IN MY CALLING OF THE LORD TO BE A SERVANT TO HIS PEOPLE, I LOVE CARING FOR THE PEOPLE IN THE COMMUNITY SUCH AS LOST SOULS, LEADING THEM TO OUR SAVIOUR THE LORD OF MY SOUL AND THE KEEPER OF MY HEART, THE CLAY MAKER AND RENEWER OF MY MIND, I HAVE THE VICYORY THROUGH HIM THAT LOVE ME, I HAVE A TESTIMONY THAT KEEPS ME ON FIRE, I AM WHO HE SAY I AM, A CHILD OF THE ALMIGHTY, PRINCE OF PEACE, THE ONLY ONE THAT CAN BE A PROVIDER, A BATTLE FIGHTER, A GIVER OF PEACE, A HEALER, MY RIGHTEOUSNESS, MY EVER PRESENT ONE, AND MY GOOD SHEPHERD, I AM GOD CHOOSEN VESSEL.

Spiritual Guidance

Be Patient with me,

My spiritual sister who minister life through their anointed songs of power, I Love You My Sister this two Artists helped me touch the hem of God's garment'

And that through their Music Ministry I push toward the mark

Tramaine Hawkins – The Potter House

Yolanda Adams – The Battle Is Not Yours

And to a very special counselor that walked through the fire with me and never let go of my hand! Kathy Melito

Book written By Evangelist Earlina Gilford - Weaver

I give God all the glory for allowing me to come out and shine among the mess, even though I was a victim of physical and sexual abuse and mental abuse.

God has birth a ministry in me to carry out nationwide so it will send the captive free

And share the victory of healing; I had suffered 35 years of not knowing that I could breathe on my own.

Hallelujah I Am Free!

Evangelist Earlina Gilford-Weaver
aka niesay7
Who Will Wipe My Tears Away?

He will wipe away every tear from their eyes,
and there will be no more death, sadness, crying
or pain, because all the old ways are gone."
Say's the One that is sitting at the throne,
Look! I am making everything NEW!
Revelation: 21 Verse 4

The Lord Is Carrying Me through It All

With all I have been through it has been a joy to know that I have revelation now, I learn how to:

Deal with emotional pain because of the abuse: Thank You Jesus

I understand my responsibility as a child of God: Thank You Jesus

I can overcome my addictive behaviors due to my past: Thank You Jesus

I know now that I have unconditional love through him that loves me "God": Thank You Jesus

I know that all things works in God's time and it will be right on time, so give him the praise while I still can: Thank You Jesus

Evangelist Earlina Gilford-Weaver

A child of the lord who had so many trials and tribulations, not Knowing her identity for half of her life, she was broken in so many pieces and did not know where and how it was Going to be put back together, even as she grew into a young adult she felt self-worth to her community. Every one she had came in contact with, shedding tears every where she went, searching for that ultimate one that would and can wipe her tears away, only digging a deeper hole for her purpose in life, through this hurt Whelming, heart breaking battle, she stopped and knock on one more doors where she found the lord in 1985 and develop a relationship with him and found love like she never had before, she finally was going to experience and feel what it takes to have the tears wiped away, and have, Earlina has been running for the Lord ever since, what a joy she has found in her life, her true and only first love,

God has given her the vision of an angel working and laboring in her true calling and true passion she had all the time, after shed one long Tear the lord heard her cry from the power she had within, she picks up her cross to carry it to the end, Sharing her testimony to all the corners of the world. East, West, South, and North, whoever the lord sends her way, Earlina gave birth to the ministries the lord had in her in 2003, with the names the lord provided, Angel W/Extra Blessing, Angel That Give Love, and God Chosen Angels, Shekinah Glory Women's Outreach Ministry, 2Real4U Drama Outreach Drama Production that blooms every day.

The Lord Jesus Christ our Savior had died on the cross just for this type of things that need to come alive because he still lives inside of us.

Earlina became an Ordain Evangelist in 2008 her passion is doing the lord work that comes from the hidden part of the body the Heart!

And to open up some Outreach ministries one day and serve God's people all over, by just being a Servant and show the true love that

Would truly help some of the tears in our generation today!

God Gets All The Glory!

God has an Angel watching out for you through every Test!

Through it all' know that the circumstances'
God is the result.

Visit our Web-Site for more Exciting Things

And to see the Movie Based' on this Novel

"Angry Tears" Filmed & Directed By David L. Walker

Visit: www.shekinahglorydrama.com

Printed in Great Britain
by Amazon